FINDERS KEEPERS

FINDERS KEEPERS

A TALE OF

ARCHAEOLOGICAL PLUNDER

AND

OBSESSION

CRAIG CHILDS

LITTLE, BROWN AND COMPANY

NEW YORK   BOSTON   LONDON

Little, Brown and Company
Hachette Book Group
237 Park Avenue, New York, NY 10017
www.hachettebookgroup.com

First Edition: August 2010

Little, Brown and Company is a division of Hachette Book Group, Inc.
The Little, Brown name and logo are trademarks of Hachette Book
Group, Inc.

Library of Congress Cataloging-in-Publication Data
Childs, Craig Leland.
    Finders keepers : a tale of archaeological plunder and obsession / Craig
Childs. — 1st ed.
        p. cm.
    Includes bibliographical references and index.
    ISBN 978-0-316-06642-6
    1. Archaeology — Moral and ethical aspects.   2. Pillage.   3. Archaeolo-
gists — Professional ethics.   4. Archaeology — Psychological aspects.
5. Archaeology — Anecdotes.   I. Title.
    CC175.C47 2010
    930.1 — dc22   2009051921

10 9 8 7 6 5 4 3 2 1

RRD-IN

Printed in the United States of America

For my dad,
his bones and ashes
scattered across the desert

Events in time are not—boom—over.
They have tentacles, and they wrap around,
and they swish back and forth,
and they sink and swim.
— AMY FUSSELMAN,
8: ALL TRUE: UNBELIEVABLE

CONTENTS

CONTENTS

Author's Note

〜〜〜〜〜〜〜〜〜〜

All characters and names in this book are real but for Art and Betty Cooper, who requested anonymity to keep their collection safe.

I frequently use the word *archaeology,* which has different meanings based on context. While it describes the scientific discipline itself, I also use the word to define the presence of archaeological material, e.g., "There was archaeology all over the place." It also refers to the larger arena surrounding artifacts, e.g., "Archaeology is one big stinking mess."

FINDERS KEEPERS

INTRODUCTION

~~~~~~~~~~~~~~~~

Her eyes looked tired, as if she had not slept in days. When I asked if she'd talk to me about her work as an archaeologist, she told me she was an unreliable source. I said not to worry, that I'd just like to hear her story. But her face worried me, and I felt like I was interviewing a vampire.

I had a beer, nothing for her. An attractive woman with a penetrating gaze, she had her legs stretched out in the booth. She had been working as a contract archaeologist documenting and clearing human remains and artifacts for a highway expansion across the Navajo reservation in northern New Mexico. She said dead people were everywhere, remains of thousands of years of occupation; the whole place was a graveyard. She and her crew would dig by day, then go back to some cheap motel room. She said that there was so much sex and drinking that now it seemed like a dream, a hedonistic foray in the land of the dead. She was raw labor in the growing field of cultural resource management, working for an environmental consulting firm that sent excavators out to clear the way for development, to pull up pots, effigies, offerings, and bones in accordance with the law. She called herself a death-eater.

Sitting at the booth she whispered, "I hate the Navajo."

"The people?" I asked.

"No, the place," she said. "The reservation."

She told me guys would come up to her, Navajo men, and tell her she should not be doing this. They said witches would come at night, steal the bones of people she was digging up, and grind them into powder that would be used in black magic rituals, hexes. She tried to reassure them by saying that when she and her colleagues found burials, the police would keep an eye on the sites until they could get them cleared out. That is when one man told her that police sell bones to witches, not enough that she would even notice, but enough to kill with. Navajo traditions are rife with death taboos and rumors of sorcery—makes sense in the Southwest, where bones are constantly weathering from the ground. The Navajo have learned you don't touch dead people's things. They aren't yours. They just bring trouble.

This is the Indiana Jones side of archaeology, the curses and chilling adventure. But in the real world, archaeologists do not believe in curses. They do their jobs. It is dirty, exhausting work and involves a lot of wind and mind-numbing ground surveys. It means construction crews are delayed, millions of dollars lost, developers watching impatiently while salvage workers dig up artifacts and skeletons. At one of her sites she found the remains of a more recently dead man, a body pitched off the side of the road. A few weeks later she found another, and she began to wonder what is the difference between someone who died months ago and someone who died a thousand years ago. Time grew thin for her, as if she could see through it. Navajos kept showing up, hitchhikers and transients telling her she better slow down with all this digging. She began to feel like a looter herself. She quit her job.

I asked if she would ever go back. She nearly cried, shaking her head, saying, "No, no, no..."

Then she straightened her face, looked at me, and said, "You know I would."

. . .

This book is about the underbelly of archaeology, from both a personal and a global perspective. It is a firsthand exploration into the many reasons we loot. To loot is to freely take something that is not yours. There are night diggers pillaging tombs and rioters with bats and crowbars pouring through the unhinged doors of the National Museum in Iraq. There are scientists who say it is looting when artifacts come without paperwork. Museum curators have called it looting when repatriation laws require them to turn over prized pieces of antiquity to faraway countries demanding their heritage back. Fingers seem to all be pointing at each other.

If you are one of those people who have strong opinions about who should own ancient cultural property and who has the right to do as they wish with antiquities, you might be surprised by your reaction to what you read here.

If you have wondered what all the fuss is about—what is so important about some clay seal lost in the desert for thousands of years—I hope this book will help you understand.

I have found myself lost in the entanglement of antiquities. From the lowliest dirt geeks to credentialed excavators to the world's biggest antiquities traffickers—all of whom you will meet in the coming pages—few hands are clean. With this formidable cast of characters working often at cross-purposes, the atmosphere can get a bit testy. Several people I began following during the writing of this book were by the end either dead or in jail. Others had only to endure the humiliation and fear of having their houses and collections raided.

In no other field of research have I encountered so many people who have wanted the other party dead. At one point I interviewed an antiquities broker—he seemed like a nice enough fellow—and a few days later heard a rumor he had put a price on the head of a troublesome foreign journalist. Another man, a pothunter now in prison, explained to an undercover agent that you should always go into the field well armed—and if law enforcement pays a visit to your digging operation, you "drop 'em...and never come back." Meanwhile, a university archaeologist has publicly implored troops to shoot people plundering archaeological sites in Iraq. On a more personal note, while I was reporting on a federal raid on looters in the Southwest, a friend sent me a note warning me to watch my back, saying the illicit artifact community was out for blood. You don't get this kind of talk from geologists or stamp collectors.

Why so much contention? We are dealing with the physical remains of all of human history. What one person takes often destroys it for another, a big gamble when we are here for such a short time, one thin layer of generations atop thousands of years of ancestry. What we do now forever changes the context of artifacts. Some see the fight over who should be able to own the physical past as a war. In order for an artifact to sit on a dealer's shelf, it must often be laundered beyond scientific recognition, the bane of archaeologists. In order for it to be in the hands of science, it is often secreted away into storage where it may never be seen again. In between are many hands scrabbling for whatever they can get.

An old Utah pothunter once took off his bracelet and

passed it to me, an inlay of silver and turquoise probably a century and a half old. "You know where I got that?" he asked. "Off a dead Navajo." The bracelet in my hands suddenly turned to ice. Though I had to swallow my own discomfort, I listened to the man whimsically explain his love for the past, saying an artifact like this is holy, physically embodying stories that take him back in time. In his mind, he was honoring the bracelet by giving it another go-round, but I remained stuck on the fact that he had driven a shovel through a nest of human bones to get it just for himself.

At the same time I, too, have dug through a human skeleton using a trowel and a brush. It was in the service of an academic excavation, and not, ostensibly, for my own edification. To say the archaeologist is right and the pothunter is wrong seems instinctive, but why?

Regardless of which players have ended up with which artifacts, we have come to the point of diminishing returns. What is left in the ground does not outweigh what has been removed. Mayan temples have been tunneled until they look like worm-eaten fruit. In China, thousands of tombs are found freshly looted every year. Parts of the Middle East look carpet bombed. Many museums, meanwhile, are stuffed until choking with objects. From arrowhead hunters to global dealers, from amateurs excavating illegally to archaeologists with university degrees picking at the ground with dental tools, we all want a piece of *it*.

Even you, dear reader, have your finger in this pie as you admire a museum's collection. Perhaps you have visited the Metropolitan Museum of Art in New York and found yourself captivated by the voluptuous statue of an Indian woman, her body polished gray-green schist and labeled a Matrika, a mother goddess, from the mid-sixth century, Tanesar, northern India. Her right hand is missing, her feet broken off. Where did this statue come from? Anand Shrivastava, a

Jaipur police superintendent dedicated to bringing down artifact smuggling rings, found a photograph of Matrikas in situ from 1961 at a shrine outside the village of Tanesar, where they had probably been in place for well over a thousand years. The shrine once had several beautifully executed Matrikas, all gone now, thought by Shrivastava to be stolen and smuggled out of the country. This particular statue surfaced when it was gifted to the Met from a private collection. The others from the shrine can now be seen in museum collections around the world. In 2003, Shrivastava traveled to the village with photographs of these missing Matrikas, asking if anyone remembered them. An old man reportedly stared at the photographs for a moment, then began to weep.

In many museums you move from one artifact to the next, and they all bear such secret stories. They are there for the sake of posterity, which, right now, is you. Enjoy.

In the debate over who should own the past, it is easy to forget what is being fought over in the first place, and from the ground up this book will be a reminder. John Carman, a leading scholar in archaeological ethics, writes, "Like it or not, by considering archaeological material as 'cultural property' we make archaeology not a handmaiden of history even, but of law and economics." What we really want from archaeology is not a debate over who owns what, but a meaningful, tangible connection to people who came long before us. We are looking for our place in time, a temporal context for our own civilization and our very lives.

I know a man who wanders parts of the Four Corners region in the American Southwest conducting archaeological surveys. Now and then he finds pre-Columbian baskets, pots, and imprinted clay tablets. Contracted by the government, he has to assess whether these artifacts are at risk of being vandalized or destroyed, and some he must help remove to federal storage for the sake of preservation. He says he would rather leave them where they are. They seem alive to him in situ, curated by sand and wind rather than by the unnerving stillness of a climate-controlled facility. He once found a weaving loom hidden in the wilderness, an intricate wooden artifact from the early centuries AD, which remained untouched in a dry, natural shelter until other people began finding it. Soon it had to be confiscated, taken to a museum so that no one else could steal it. The man understood why this had to happen, but the loom's absence felt like a strange shadow in the world, a nitpicking emptiness. So, he carefully studied the loom, and after fastidious work constructed a replica. It did not have the same greased tarnish as the original, but was measured exactly, its many long, thin dowels tied together with twine and little knots. He walked his creation into the desert and placed it where the first loom had been, giving the shadow an object back.

This is not simply a book of violations. It is a book of choices. It is how we answer the conundrum of archaeology, the moral questions it poses. Consciously or not, most of us have already made our choices. This book will help you understand why you made yours.

PART ONE

~~~~~~~~~~~~~~~~~~~~~

IN THE COUNTRY OF THE DEAD

CHAPTER I

AMATEURS

I grew up spitting on potsherds. I would find them on the dry, gravelly earth of south-central Arizona—pieces of broken bowls, jars, and water ollas dating back several hundred years. Rubbing spit around with my thumb, I would clean off the dirt to see if there might be a fragment of a design underneath, part of a red spiral or maybe the head of a waterbird painted with a human-hair brush. The prettier the design, the longer I held it, as if it were an eye opening in my hand, staring out from the other end of time.

My dad used to take me hunting in the desert, and we would find pottery on gentle mounds or exposed at the cut of an arroyo. He would go down on one knee, the butt of his 12-gauge resting on the ground, his fingers sorting through ancient trash left from an era when huts and adobe fortresses once stretched across this country. It was not really trash, not in the way we think of it. People here used to bury their dead in rubbish mounds, not stuffing bodies in randomly but interring them with a full complement of vessels and jewelry made of shell and turquoise. Trash was a part of their social architecture, a claim on the ground. You could walk up to a site centuries later and know exactly who had lived there based on what they left in front of their settlements; who they traded with, what they made themselves, what kind of wares they employed in their kitchens. These refuse piles, their surfaces now winnowed down to just stone and pottery, are the stories of actual lives.

I would watch my dad closely, matching his motions, leaning my .22 barrel against my shoulder as I searched for the right sherd to pick up, a big curve the cattle had not crushed and modern pickers had not taken. I learned to stand up with one I liked and admire it for a moment, just as he did, before flicking it to the ground like a bottle cap, or a coin winged into a fountain.

If he ever took one home, I never saw it. Had my dad been a pothunter, I would have been one too, happily booting a shovel into the ground right next to him. But he was not. It was enough for him to imagine people buried under his feet, funerary vessels encircling their heads as he walked by. He liked to talk about *mystery* and *the lay of things.* Then, we would find a car battery someone had junked out in the desert, and if there had not been any luck with quail or cottontail, we would take aim and blow the crap out of the thing. It was our contribution to archaeology. If the belly-ruptured remains of a battery ever survived for a thousand years, someone might find them and be able to look back and see the two of us out on a Sunday afternoon, 1977.

The general cutoff for archaeology is sixty years. Before that, it is trash, after that, an artifact. In a way, this is an arbitrary line, but sixty years is about the time when objects begin to fade from living memory. Even ugly things become beautiful after sixty years. What may have once been commonplace becomes rare. A forgotten vessel, such as a bottle or a jar, turns into a time machine. A piece of glass or pottery opens a keyhole to look through.

The lives of these artifacts do not begin when they are lifted from the ground, or when you first make eye contact with them in a museum case. They begin centuries, even millennia, earlier, when they are first conceived—a potter fashioning a vessel from riverbed clay, an artisan polishing tiny shell beads for a necklace, later to be worn, then lost, maybe found again. They each carry private, human histories. Usually we see them in climate-controlled rooms, dust-free display cases, where it can be difficult to imagine where they came from. This is not the same as seeing them in their place, where they were left. In situ, an object is far more than just itself. It becomes the horizon and the whole sky, and the occasional whip of a breeze where my father and I would walk, stopping along the way to peer back through time. The past becomes an entire landscape, a country. In order to understand why it has a hold on us, and why we sometimes have bitterly different responses to how we treat it, one needs to come to the ground and see where it all begins both physically and emotionally.

. . .

By my early twenties I was eating jackrabbits and wiping my ass with rocks, a free man in the wilderness. Indeed, if ever awards were given to folks of my ilk, unaffiliated backcountry aficionados, I would have had my Eagle Scout badge. For money I got a job taking high school kids from Los Angeles into the desert. The company paid seventy-five dollars a day, good wages for a ratty bunch of guides working desolate country around the lower Colorado River between Arizona, Nevada, California, and Mexico. We taught basic outdoor skills, and we called ourselves naturalists. Mostly in our twenties and thirties, we were burgeoning scientists and misanthropes, each bringing to the table some appreciable field skill. One could heal injuries and cure sicknesses with local plants she knew by their Latin names; another excelled at finding potable water in the most forbidding terrain. There were those who could start fires with hand drills, those who caught small creatures with snares. I was the archaeology guy, finding rock art and little bits of fascination on the ground.

On our days off we scavenged food from the company van and headed out together to set up quick camps and climb bareback ridges for no reason other than the sun and the hard scrape of the earth. Dressed in threadbare T-shirts or sports bras, we were tanned and scabbed and exquisite.

Midday on one of these excursions we found a rocky alcove out of the sun and the six of us piled into its shade. We lowered packs off our shoulders, uncapped water bottles. Right away the place looked familiar, lived in. Sharper rocks had been cleared out of the way, and the low ceiling had a bit of fire-black, a sign that the shelter had been used by fire builders. I ran my hand across the ground where I found dry, hard nuts of bighorn sheep droppings. Between them was a small seashell, a little *Olivella* like a curl of white paper.

A seashell in the middle of the desert means a lot. The nearest place to pick one up is the coast some 150 miles away in Mexico. For well over a thousand years people had traveled across dunes and arid horizons to fill baskets with shells. They were a primary trade resource for the prehistoric Southwest, moving along organized routes where traders lived off of water caches, globelike ollas they had left in the sand, or rare natural waterholes that they decorated with rock art. The shells they carried were traded inland sometimes as far as 600 miles. This one was left behind.

"Check this out," I said, holding it up for all to see. "Dead people."

The others gathered around the shell as if I had found a diamond. It just takes one little thing to send my mind reeling. I saw copper-skinned people filing between isolated mountains, baskets weighted across their foreheads on leather tumps. They had bare legs, hard footsoles, and spun countless generations of themselves before asphalt or steel ever came to this land. They used to pour shells into graves as offerings and made them into jewelry. In good times, when civilization was running high, these shells passed through by the millions (at one Southwestern archaeological site researchers counted 3.9 million imported shells). Certain villages acted as production centers where artisans worked them into pendants or fetishes, carved and polished them, decorated them with precious stones. From there the shells moved into high-profile pueblos built like citadels across the landscape. All of this you see in one object, something small as a thumbnail.

We each began combing the ground. I found a few more shells. Bone beads started coming up, each hardly bigger than the polished head of a pin. One guide was methodically picking beads from the sand, crouching and hopping from one to the next, resting them two at a time on the skin of his thumb before cupping them and hunting for more. He collected a handful, then stopped to count them, quietly thrilling to his addition.

I watched him for a while, then asked, "You aren't going to take those, are you?"

He looked up at me from under his wild, blond mop. From nights spent in Yuma together I knew him as a boxing drunkard, and from the field as a competent, intuitive traveler. We had stayed up nights talking about stars and miracles, and he was a good few inches taller than me.

"Aw, man, don't start that," he said.

"Come on," I complained. "They've been here forever, just leave them."

The others said nothing.

Gut reactions do not come from reason or deliberation.

They are an instant reaction of the heart. Mine said the beads should stay. I felt that the cave would lose a bit of its magic if he took them.

"They're *beads*," the blond man said. "You know, *trade beads*. It's what beads are for. They *go*."

"What about their context—this shelter, this desert? They belong here."

He closed his fist on the beads and said, "I *am* their context."

I sighed. I had to let go. Arguing any further would just create animosity, not something I wanted on a walk with friends.

I waved my hand in the air, saying, "OK, OK."

He retired to the back of the alcove, admiring his find, and I watched the sun move outside, wishing I knew the words to put the beads back.

. . .

To truly unravel the dilemmas of archaeology, there are many parts of the equation to understand. Why do we take things? Why do we leave them?

James O. Young has written eloquently on the competing claims over ownership. Chair of the Department of Philosophy at the University of Victoria in British Columbia, Young takes a frank and principled approach to archaeology, saying that artifacts ultimately belong to the cultures that made them. That is, they belong to these cultures if they are proven to have had a genuine, substantial, and enduring significance to the people. If they aren't so significant, it's finders keepers. For instance, a member of the Hopi Cultural Protection Office says that even a digging stick, one that might be found in a cave, is culturally significant, sacred in fact, and belongs in Hopi custody. Young contends that cultures cannot rightly claim every single thing produced by past members.

It would be untenable, a flood coming out of museums, private collections, and all those who bought trinkets at roadside stands or found them lying on the ground. We would all have to shake out our pockets to return what has been picked up.

In Young's view, smaller or less important artifacts—like a random bead—are subject to the discretion of whoever finds them (depending on local laws, of course). Young writes of an arrowhead that his mother dug from her garden in suburban Vancouver, one now on his mantel: "It has no particular significance to any aboriginal culture. If it were a rare and unusually beautiful example, or had considerable ritual significance, the situation might be different. As it is, I do not act wrongly in keeping it. I own it."

When I asked about his decision to keep the object, Young replied, "The arrowhead was in a state of nature. Keeping it would be no different than picking a flower that grew wild in my garden. If it were an item of huge cultural significance, the situation could be different."

But huge cultural significance is not easily quantifiable. Who decides? He continued, "If I found the artifact in a park or other public property, I think that I would offer it to some public body."

This is almost a universal response: find something and pick it up, and if reasonable ethics prevail you turn it over to the proper authorities, handing it to a park ranger who is likely mystified as to why people keep grabbing objects and handing them in, filling so many drawers and boxes it seems a waste. It is as if we cannot stand to leave things the way we find them. There is a widespread assumption that removing an artifact is preferred, whether you take it for yourself or not. Jimmy Carter, when he was president, amended a crucial antiquities act so that it would have a loophole for arrowheads. Being an arrowhead collector himself, Carter wanted to make sure you could still scratch one out of the dirt and take it home, connecting yourself with the history of your country by owning a piece of it. (Carter's clause does not legalize arrowhead-hunting on public lands, but merely says that one cannot be penalized for it under the Archaeological Resources Protection Act of 1979. One can be penalized under other laws, however, meaning it is still illegal.)

I took the question of ownership to Randy Cohen, who writes a weekly ethics column for the *New York Times Magazine*. Cohen answered smoothly: "In ethics, truly abandoned property, by which I mean something deliberately abandoned or that can't be reunited with its owner, is in fact up for grabs. It follows the finders keepers rule. So, if you see a $20 bill on the street you've got as much claim to it as anybody, if there is no way you can reunite it with its owner. But if you find a guy's wallet and it has some ID in it, you can't keep it. You have to make a good faith effort to return it. And so the question with antiquities then becomes well, is there a legitimate owner? And in my view there is. Cultures have a claim on their significant objects."

And when the bloodlines that made the artifacts are long gone, as was arguably the case for the beads in the rock shelter? Cohen argues that there is a kind of continuity that makes the locality where the artifacts are found a stand-in for the owner. They should remain in place. He told me, "There is much to be said for keeping archaeological works in the location where they are found, because their meaning is often very much tied into place. It's a really good thing that the pyramids are still in Egypt. Our understanding of them is aided by that, deepened by that. So that becomes a kind of argument for keeping it there."

Cohen asked what I do with my finds, and I told him I leave them there. I might take a picture or make a sketch in my journal, but I don't tell anyone where they are. I prefer to walk away and let time fill back in behind me. Too much has been taken already. We don't need any more. I have been in the bowels of museums around the country, and the sheer volume of artifacts sitting in dark storage is overwhelming. Enough is enough.

"That's an interesting way to look at it," Cohen said. "I don't have a counterargument to that. Once there's an excess of this kind of stuff it gets very tricky. What do you imagine happens to what you leave behind?"

"If somebody else finds it, it's probably gone," I said.

. . .

When the heat of day drifted off, we emerged from the cave and walked. The sky fell to sunset. A gibbous moon passed over us into the evening, unveiling pale shadows of saguaros and cholla. We traveled across vacant magma fields, dark rhyolitic char brought up from inside the earth. When the night grew too long, we set a scattered camp. The bead stealer and I sat up and watched the stars.

Though it was not what I wanted, I said, "Maybe you're right. Maybe the beads were meant to travel."

After all, I tried to convince myself, they were only beads, perhaps a small thing to quibble over. I certainly didn't find Young at fault for keeping an arrowhead his mother found in the garden.

"Maybe," my companion agreed.

Neither of us really knew.

Legally, he was not allowed to take those beads. In the United States, it has been illegal to remove artifacts without permission from public lands since 1906. That 1906 law reads that in order to "appropriate, excavate, injure, or destroy any historic or prehistoric ruin or monument, or any object of antiquity, situated on lands owned or controlled by the Government of the United States," one must have government permission.

In the open desert, however, other laws applied. Older laws. Conscience and gut reaction. There was no government but the elements, no secretaries but us.

In the morning we broke camp and flushed into the desert like birds. We moved quickly, coming down from mountains into boulder-bottomed arroyos. Shadows cleared out as the afternoon heat came on. Our movements slowed. The sun seemed to have halted, a marble stopped in the bowl of the sky. As our rest stops became longer, I scanned the horizon with a pair of field glasses and spotted a bit of shadow rippling half a mile away.

"There," I said. "A cave."

We changed course, crossed a field of bony ocotillos over a ridge. The cave was up a slope of broken rock, hard to spot, just a wink of shade. When we climbed inside, it was as if we were stepping into a ballroom. Our shadows danced into an enclosure much larger than I had expected. One of the guides set off running, making gymnastic leaps with her arms thrown outward. Elegant scarves of dust sailed behind her.

"We could live in this place," another said, his voice boosted to echo through the room.

The ceiling was made of domed bedrock that emitted a faint hum, an echo of dust devils riding across the desert far away. I walked in and crouched over beetle tracks in the dust, tiny notations. It was an undisturbed space, centuries of powdery accumulation. Beneath the dust were subtle shapes, as if a deep snow had fallen on sleeping figures. As I walked farther, I tested my weight, pressing into a desiccated sponge of buried wood-rat droppings and cactus needles. Below were muted spaces, loose fill. It was in caves like this that people used to live and bury their dead, not just a day's stopover but an actual habitation site.

"People are buried in here," I said.

The others stopped, looked around, let their eyes adjust. Judging by the size of the cave, it must have been an important place, a grand shelter probably used for 10,000 years, and beneath us lay unseen graves, skeletons supine, surrounded by whatever offerings were given to them. Usually you would find a cave like this and it would be a war zone of looters' pits, yet there was not even a quick cathole in here.

In the 1930s, the eminent Southwest archaeologist Emil Haury and his field-hardened sidekick Julian Hayden excavated a similar-looking place, Ventana Cave, also in southern Arizona. They came out with Stone Age utensils and textiles, Neolithic pottery and jewelry, all highly preserved by the region's aridity. Ventana Cave dates from Paleo-Indians to Indians, a rare view into continuous human history from the eighth millennium BC onward. They found the skeleton of an infant bundled inside a twine bag and placed in a nest of grass, and near that more adult burials with quivers and arrows, shell pendants, necklaces. A mummified man was unearthed with earrings still hanging from the flaps of his earlobes and a clay plug piercing his nose. It was not just the dead that came out. One of the cleanest records of North American occupation was exhumed from that cave, its contents painstakingly illustrated, measured, photographed, and installed in museum storage.

Emil Haury isn't the only man who explored caves like this one. There are also men like Jack Harelson, a former insurance agent who fancied himself an amateur archaeologist. His house was heavily stocked with illegally obtained artifacts he had either picked up or dug, including one of the oldest pair of sandals ever found in North America (around 10,000 years old).

Harelson's biggest dig was Elephant Mountain Cave, an expansive natural shelter in Nevada's Black Rock Desert, its mouth partly obscured by scrub and boulders. He excavated the site in the 1980s, spent several years privately removing the floor with shovels and screens. It was his own personal Atlantis. Among the many hundreds of artifacts he recovered, Harelson dug up a 2,000-year-old sealed torso-sized basket, heavy with objects inside. Showing at least some restraint, he left the basket unopened until he got it back to his garage, invited some friends over, and peeled it open before them. He pulled out a bowl, a knife, and a net used to catch rabbits. Under that was a mummified boy who had been about four years old when he died, and below his leathery corpse was another mummy, that of a girl about ten years old with long black hair, her body tucked knees to chest.

At a later point the mummies' heads were pulled off, the bodies bagged and buried in Harelson's backyard.

For his part in this Harelson was caught and jailed in 1996, hit with eighteen months in prison. Two thousand objects were confiscated from his house. Harelson defended himself by saying he was an amateur archaeologist and that he intended to hand over the material to a museum when he was finished. (He had produced other finds before—mammoth bones donated to the Nevada State Museum, for example. But turning over artifacts would have implicated him in a crime.)

Harelson's fine was a record-breaking $2.5 million—$750,000 for restoration and repair of the cave, and $1.75 million for the scientific and cultural value destroyed by his excavation. As he passed down this heavy sentence, the judge in the case was heard to say, "You are not an amateur archaeologist. You are a common thief." (Harelson, incensed, later hired a hit man and made a list of those he wanted killed: the judge, the lead officer in the case, two former business partners, and his ex-wife, who had handed over incriminating evidence. Harelson paid for the first kill with $10,000 in raw opals, but the man he hired turned out to be an undercover agent. Harelson was sentenced to a further ten years in prison.)

I walked the breadth of the cave we had found, well aware of why Harelson is vilified and Haury and Hayden have been celebrated. One made collection a private pleasure, taking history for himself. The others added their finds to a greater body of knowledge, now accessible through libraries and museums. The distance between these two ends of the spectrum seems like forever, but it is not.

In the back of the cave was an oval-shaped enclosure, a natural vestibule. I stepped into it and found Irvin, a fellow guide known for digging up grubs for eating. He was standing before a pyramid of stacked rock. The pile was waist high and slowly being reclaimed by the earth, flushed in centuries of dust. I walked up beside him.

"Kind of out of place," Irvin said.

"Shrine," I said. Why a shrine? Why else would people put a neat, tall rock pile back here? It was something special, *ceremonial*, as many archaeologists would say.

"Well, let's see," Irvin said. He rolled up his sleeve, got down on his knees, and shoved his arm into a wood-rat burrow at the base of the pyramid. He went nearly up to his shoulder, his cheek pressed into soft blow-sand.

"Rattlesnakes," I warned.

He puffed dust away from his mouth and said, "I know."

"What's in there?" I asked.

He was concentrating, feeling around. I wanted it to be my hand reaching into the ground, but I did not have the brazenness. He came out holding a fistful of dust and a short wooden rod only slightly longer and fatter than a pencil. It had sinew wrapped around it. Irvin looked at the object for a moment and then handed it to me before sticking his arm back down the hole.

The sinew had turned brittle. There were stripes of red paint, a hematite pigment.

"It's a painted arrow shaft." I laughed in surprise. The Patayan people, who likely put it here several centuries ago, were no-nonsense desert types, rarely dabbling in decoration. This was a rare find. Irvin's hand was rummaging around in the archaeological record, looking for more, upsetting the lay of strata that would help a researcher if this place were ever excavated. But it was a wood-rat burrow, and I figured rodents had already been churning up the record, probably denning in coils of baskets down there.

The other guides started coming around, asking what we were doing. I passed them the arrow.

Next Irvin came out with a wooden stub. He passed it up and I blew off dust—another painted projectile. This was a hunting shrine, had to be. Rituals would have been held in this cave, maybe a particularly potent hunter buried here.

In many of the old cultures, hunting is a sacred act. Among the San people of South Africa, when a man shoots a poison arrow into an eland, he bridges himself into the animal. It may take days to track down the dying eland, and during that time people are quiet around the hunter so that the prey will not be startled. He drinks little, tries not to urinate so that the animal will also not urinate and expel the poison. If it is a first-time kill, a young hunter will start a fire and use its ash to draw a circle on his forehead and a line down his nose, the same markings as those on the face of the eland.

No doubt the Patayans whose cave we had entered gave such detailed motions to their hunt. The same families may have lived in this region for over a thousand years, enough time to entrench their traditions, except rather than eland, Patayans would have pursued bighorn sheep. They are known to have set fire to bighorn carcasses in what were likely ritual acts, leaving behind charred skulls and horns stacked upon each other in the open desert. Little is known about these people, partly because universities that establish summer field camps prefer the higher, cooler parts of the state. What is known is that they buried their dead in caves and on the graves built cook fires and sleeping platforms, adding layers of their lives to the ground.

Now their offerings were in my hands. We passed them around, fireworks going off in our imaginations. These were not beads spilled accidentally in a rock shelter. These had been put here as offerings. I trusted the people around me, even the bead stealer. We all knew this was different. The objects inside the rock stack had been painted and lowered into the ground, maybe settled on the chest of a dead man Irvin was reaching around.

After making the circle, each artifact was returned to Irvin, who placed it back inside. We were somewhere between Harelson and Haury; curious, perhaps meddlesome, but not intending to take anything.

I wanted more, though. I knew there was more. I was caught up in the elation of discovery, my eye fixed on the pyramid itself. I wondered if it had some interior chamber such as those inside stupas in India or chortens in Tibet. It looked easy to uncap. I felt hesitation in my body, a sense of trespass, but my curiosity was overwhelming. I told myself that we would leave this place exactly as it was. Only a moment's disruption, and we'd be gone.

I reached out and grabbed the flat, heavy topstone and lifted it off. I set it on the ground as dust spilled into a space inside the pyramid.

Irvin got off his knees and looked in, our heads touching. A nest of shadowy wooden objects lay within, and for a moment I just stared like it was a bottomless well, nothing but time down there. I reached in, touched one, lifted it out. It felt dry and old.

It was a bow, but made small, a miniature. I had never seen such a thing in the wild. It would have been a representational object, certainly an offering. Along its sides were etchings, lines and hatchwork. A shiver started at the back of my neck and spread around my body, as if gaps between centuries were closing.

The other guides stared at the bow in my hands. A bunch of Tom Sawyers and Huck Finns we were, enchanted by what a person might find in a cave. Irvin took the bow from me, studied it, and grinned with amazement. He handed it to someone else as I dislodged another, and then another, each with a different sign etched or painted on it.

I envisioned people gathered here, ceremonies invoking animal spirits, calling for a good hunt. The Patayans were here before reservations, before the Spanish and their horses, before guns. Dating back at least to the early centuries AD and probably long before that, the people who occupied the desert surrounding the lower Colorado River moved seasonally, growing crops along the river, hunting and gathering in the desert beyond. We were well within their migration range, a place they would have come to in the spring while their temporary encampments were being washed out by annual river floods. This cave would have been a key location, a place to take shelter for a period, or a place where young men came to mark their first kill.

"These are cool," someone said, letting loose a laugh that somehow sounded mean. I looked up. I knew him only as an ugly man with an expansive, ratty beard and an unstable character. He was new to the company, and this was the first time he and I had ever walked in the desert together.

"I mean, it's a real bow," he said. "A real Indian bow. Have you ever seen one of these before?"

I said, "No, not out here."

He looked at me and said, "You can't tell me we have to leave these."

My mouth was open. I needed a drink of water badly.

"I think they should stay, yes," I said, my lips gummy with thirst.

"Get off your shit," Ugly Man replied.

"I don't think we should be stealing from a shrine," I said.

"That's pussy talk." He glowered, making sure I did not get an edge on him. He had heard me with the bead stealer and knew I would be easy. "These people have been dead forever. When was the last time anyone was here? I mean, really? It's been hundreds of years. You think they remember this place? They don't."

Earlier in the day Ugly Man and I had had a small altercation, and he had threatened to brain me with a rock. I had stared back at him dumbfounded, not sure what to say. He radiated aggression. I had to be careful. A fistfight in a cave full of hunting magic and ancient dead would not be good. And for me, a fight with Ugly Man would not end well. Though American born, he had just gotten out of the Israeli army, fighting Palestinians house to house. I, however, was raised mostly by a single mother and have a predilection for flowers.

"It's a shrine," I complained again.

He wagged the bow at me. "Listen, somebody else is going to find this. How could they not? And they'll take all these bows just like that."

"You want to take them instead?"

"Better us than them." He glanced around to see who was with him, but nobody was. Ugly Man cocked his jaw. "Come on, there's nothing wrong with it."

Trying to answer him, I felt like I was stammering,

empty-handed. I had no argument for how I felt, other than that we should not take these things. They are not ours. But I had never had to come up with a reason why.

The day before, I had given up on the beads much easier, but this transgression felt a level deeper. Professor Young would have said that this was culturally significant and probably would have felt a justifiable responsibility to report it to officials, something I would not do for fear of the cave being excavated and its contents moved into storage. Randy Cohen would have called the cave a stand-in for the rightful owners and probably done the same as Young. What would I do?

I blurted, "Finders keepers."

Ugly blinked as if confused. But he knew I had him. Being the finder of these bows, I got to say what happened to them. He studied the bow in his hands, my words more potent than a double dare.

"Oh, come on," he said in disbelief. "Really?"

He glanced around again and saw he still had no supporters. It would have shamed him to take the bow outright, with nobody believing in him. He was in the wrong crowd and had to suck it in, looking at the cave ceiling, letting out a frustrated breath.

"OK, whatever," he said. "You can keep your bow." Later, I couldn't get the rotten taste out of my mouth. Even as we dispersed to our own parts of the cave, each taking a bow to study in silence, I felt I had opened a door I should have left closed. I sat with my journal, my private room of drawings and words, sketching bows and arrows on clean, white paper, but I had trouble concentrating. When the shadows began tilting outside, it was time to go. Each person set a bow or two at the foot of the shrine. I gathered them and placed them back just as I had roughly sketched them from memory, the one with zigzags above the one etched with lines. It might matter how they were placed, I thought.

One seemed to be missing.

I had not thought to count them to start with, and now I wasn't sure. The cache felt that much smaller, though. I looked behind me, saw everybody readying for departure. Ugly was stuffing something in his pack, having trouble making it fit. He got the thing in, slung his pack onto his shoulders, and moved for the entrance. Before he was out he checked his back, saw me watching him, and quickly looked away. I knew it then for sure: He had screwed me. He was making off with a bow.

My brain kept shouting as I watched him leave, *Do something, do something, do something!* But I had no plea that would convince him. Short of my stealing the bow back, which could involve physical violence, there was nothing I could do. The bow was now his.

What does it mean that we take memories out of the ground like this, permanently emptying the land piece by piece? In describing the spiritual and physical landscape of North America, N. Scott Momaday once wrote that over the course of thousands of years of occupation people "died into the ground again and again and so made it sacred." By one bow, this cave had now been unhallowed.

It felt like winter inside me. I was the one who had spotted this place to begin with, who had uncapped the small pyramid, and who had let the bow escape. I felt like a thief. I had to be more careful about my actions and the fine lines of ethics around me. It is, after all, only a matter of scale among beads, bows, and who knows what else. I reached out and put the topstone back, sealing the chamber, cutting my losses. I turned and walked out of the cave, where I was branded by sunlight. The desert opened the way it always does, welcoming all sinners.

CHAPTER 2

THE DESTINY JAR

It is difficult to know the right thing to do, or to even imagine there is a steadfast right or wrong when it comes to antiquities. A benign act in one sense becomes a trespass in another. I once observed an archaeological field survey where students were planting colored pin-flags at every artifact they located on the ground: potsherds, arrowheads, square nails, bits of porcelain, a curl of black leather from a shoe. The earth around them seemed busy with generations and cultures, made even more so by this fresh forest of calf-high markers. Researchers called numbers back and forth, checking off lines on a clipboard as they measured distances between specimens, recording every placement and relationship, a consummate record of context. The entire site could then be reconstructed in the lab, layers of time cross-referenced. At the end of the day, they packed every small find into bags and boxes and carried them away, a procedure known as a surface collection, or, to some, hoovering. Everything was sucked up. I later walked through this naked acre of land and it seemed as if nothing human-related had ever happened here, like a plug of history had been pried out. It felt dispirited and eerie. No students I spoke with had any reservation about what they were doing, and I, too, believed it was for a good cause—the accumulation of greater knowledge—but the end result was the same as everywhere else, a piece of emptiness left behind.

The removal of things from their places happens in so many ways, both meticulous and reckless, legal and not, that it feels like a flood coming off the land, a tide rolling back and exposing nothing. I have found empty territories out there, regions riddled with so many holes, spoil piles, and blown-open graves that the past seems mined. The feeling of violation is not limited to North American archaeology. I have felt the same uneasiness in Honduras, seeing the overgrown mouth of a looter's tunnel in the side of a Mayan temple, and in Tibet, standing inside a lonely, ruined monastery where I found the floor pilfered into craters. It is how we treat history as a whole, willing to do anything to get it into our hands.

I once took some climbing rope into the east-central Arizona uplands and spent a season crossing the Apache reservation, north of the Black River, where I found cliff dwellings stacked inside vaulted canyons. It took days to get back in there, and I worked hard tracking cliff walls with binoculars or on the ground hunting for a telltale potsherd. The pottery led up, like a trail marker, to cliff dwellings overhead, and every one I found was empty. Most had been hit by pothunters, dirt floors dug wide open to get at burials underneath where the best artifacts can be found. Some digs had been smoothed over by archaeologists as if they had left a clean sheet over their excavations, most of their specimens now in storage at the Arizona State Museum. The land slowly changed for me as I found one cleared site after the next. No matter how thoroughly I searched, just about every site was disturbed, if not by diggers and shovels, then by people pawing with bare hands, leaving only crumbs of broken artifacts, corncobs, and gray, undecorated potsherds.

The people who used to live here are now known as Salado, manufacturers of bold polychrome vessels and fine loom-woven textiles. It is not even known what they actually called themselves, and though a careful search of the country reveals ancient boundary markers in rock art and ceramic styles, there is no defined area belonging to any particular people. They are dead and gone, and their physical memory has no defense other than various federal and state laws saying that their artifacts are a national heritage, U.S. property, and are thus not to be removed but by government decree.

A month after coming out of the wilderness, I was still wondering where it had all gone, imagining countless possibilities of curators, closets, and trash cans. That was when I walked into a reading room in a building a few states away from Arizona. With a book in my hand, looking for a place to sit, I noticed a display case full of dusty-looking objects on the other side of the room. I walked to it, and what I saw brought me up against the glass. Inside were so many whole pots it looked like a Mexican market. The colorful styles pinned down the location: they came from where I had been traveling. They were Salado. I wasn't sure whether I should be more astonished by the coincidence or by how out of place they seemed. The only description was written in pencil on an index card.

These came from Arizona.

Looking closer, I saw one of the lesser pots had been split in two and then put back together. It was a classic pothunter's mistake, a shovel driven straight through the center.

"You son of a bitch," I muttered, shaking my head, almost laughing with disbelief. Someone got away with this archaeological loot, grew too old to hang on to it, and gave it to a public institution to care for. The institution did not know what to do with it, so they stuck it in a reading room with a vague note explaining its provenance.

I felt I had to do something to lean against this flood. Without much thought, I hatched a plan.

. . .

I carefully scoped out the reading room to see when it received the least traffic, and two weeks later entered with a satchel, a knife, and a bandana. My heart was beating up in my throat. The last time I had done anything like this, I was fourteen. I shoplifted a toothbrush from a neighborhood drugstore and barely made it to the exit without emptying my bladder on myself. I had vowed never to do anything like it again. Now I was in my midtwenties, and the stakes were much higher.

I moved quietly between tables and chairs. The lights were off. I kept swallowing my spit even though I didn't have any. I checked the doorway over my shoulder, and checked it again. No one there. I went to the display case and took out my knife, thinking, *Make this quick*. I pressed the stone-sharpened blade into the molding and peeled it all the way around until the glass came out easily in my hands. I used the bandana to lower it to the floor, making sure not to leave fingerprints.

I reached in, snaked my hand between fat multicolored jars—clean, colorful specimens that could sell for a couple of thousand dollars on the open market. I picked the one split in half. It was smaller, less obvious, the size and shape of a cantaloupe, painted with red, white, and black designs. It was the one that seemed the most violated. A fine mist of dust had gathered on its shoulders. My fingers spanned it as I lifted it into the open where I could see the damage more clearly, the inside webbed with masking tape and hard gobs of craft glue, evidence of a cheap, inexperienced repair job.

A band of thieves we are, pillagers of time. One person stole this pot from the ground, and now I was taking it back. No paperwork, no drawn-out legal battles—this uncatalogued collection shoved off in the corner was not on anyone's radar. So I was going to repatriate it myself. Who else knew the canyons of its origin better than I? I slipped the vessel into my satchel.

Inside the case, the absence was obvious, a gap left on a shelf. I reached in with the bandana and rearranged the remaining pots until they looked evenly spread, leaving faint circles in the dust. I leaned in my head and blew across the row of pots. The dust danced up and settled.

I took only one artifact from the case, a truly symbolic gesture, considering how unlikely it was that anyone would even notice it gone. As far as I could ascertain, the pothunter had lived for a brief time in the 1950s in Arizona, where he probably enjoyed going out with a shovel over his shoulder, an amateur archaeologist. This time he had hit gold with a fourteenth-century Salado-culture burial site. He likely kept the artifacts in his house until his wife demanded that he move the dusty prizes out to the garage. Eventually he died, and then his wife died, and his children were left holding the bag. They donated the small collection to a public body, no name or plaque to go with it.

I lifted the glass, seated it, worked the molding with the backside of my knife blade so it appeared undamaged and firmly held the glass in place. My knife went back in my satchel and I turned for the doorway, then down a hall to a winding stairwell. Then I remembered the alarm. A pair of sensors hung on either side of the exit doors and could be set off by something as subtle as a magnetic strip stuck into the masking tape. Why would they tag an old, broken artifact like this? Earlier I had dismissed the possibility, but now, peering at the two big doors in the distance, I began questioning my logic. If I tripped the alarm, these halls would ring. Would I bolt or freeze? I imagined myself just standing in place, my face looking dumb as a dark stain spread down my pants.

I tried not to think about it. I walked faster, but the doors felt as if they were receding. Or maybe I was becoming smaller. I reached out as far as my arm would stretch and pushed against a brass plate. The door opened.

The alarm did not trigger.

I stepped outside and eased the door closed behind me, soft click. In cool, open air I turned and the morning sun touched my face.

. . .

I once spoke with an old Zen master named Sheng-yen, who had returned a stolen seventh-century Buddha head to its shrine in China. He had been given the head as a gift by lay followers (purchased for around $1 million on the New York antiquities market), and when he saw fresh cut marks on its neck, he knew that there was a grotesquely damaged statue somewhere. Sheng-yen invited archaeologists to study this gift until they determined its source, and he took it back. At a Chinese monastery, in a crowded ceremony, the head was returned to the shoulders of a serenely seated statue known as Akshyoba, the Imperturbable Buddha.

Speaking through a translator in Taiwan, Sheng-yen told me he returned the head out of sadness. When it was in his possession, he thought about people who had seen this statue centuries before him and how they made sculptures to venerate the Buddha, and he could not bear leaving things broken the way they were.

It was a reaction similar to mine in Salado territory and at the display case where I first saw this jar. Something had been terribly severed.

I took the jar to the Apache reservation. I had a place in mind, a network of canyons. Dark of night, several days into the reservation, I was awake listening to the breathing of two companions in nearby sleeping bags. They were along to help me with this journey, dead asleep after another long day of walking. I crawled from my bag, went for my pack, and pulled out the jar. I took it behind a boulder and flicked on my headlamp.

I could not hear anything but the rub of my clothing. It was silent and winter cold. The three of us had been walking many miles of cascading, boulder-filled canyons to get back this far.

Squatting with a headlamp, I studied the jar's broad, open mouth, its round body meticulously painted with designs. I wondered if all the hands that had ever passed across it were somehow stored in the clay in the same way solidifying liquid holds sound waves. Somewhere in this vessel there was a room inside a cliff dwelling—a firelit space with a hard-packed floor, low ceiling, smoke-blackened beams. I'd seen enough to imagine what it would have been like.

The jar came from a time when this area was both a contested landscape and a cultural melting pot for most of the Southwest. It was before Cowboys and Indians, before Apaches and Navajos. This is older history: the famously disappeared Anasazi in the north had just disbanded, vacating most of their settlements and sending an exodus of migrants outward. It is believed that many took up residence in this part of Arizona and mixed with local groups to become the Salado, using secluded canyons for guard posts and high citadels. Population centers erupted across the countryside, large, red-walled pueblos ringed by moats of canyons. It was a Tolkienesque scene of masonry compounds and fortresses in the cliffs.

As I slowly turned the jar I searched back beyond the pot-hunter and his shovel, back to hands setting it into a grave near the head of a corpse stretched out beneath turquoise and shell offerings. Before it had been buried, I imagined a woman setting out this jar at a meal, the painted designs an attractive addition to the room.

Colorful, decorated vessels are not just pretty pots, they are pieces of social architecture. In their designs and styles you would have known who the owners were trading with, what region their family came from, and perhaps even what societies and phratries they belonged to. (Women buried in this area have been found with an abundance of northern wares, which suggests that they married their way south, bringing ceramics with them.)

In my years of traveling the Southwest, I would read messages on the ground in potsherds and in partial vessels exposed in open washes or spilled from high doors of cliff dwellings. I was always struck by how they changed from one physiogeographic region to the next: in the north were bold black-on-white ceramics in tight-painted geometry and to the south reds and buffs with highly stylized figures of humans and animals. These objects are calling cards from home landscapes. When they are removed, the markers of those places are lost. We look down to see who has been here before us, the knowledge not simply for our own edification but for a transmission from the past, a voice for those who once occupied this land. When we look down and they are gone, so are the people.

With almost every last marker taken, I wanted to bring one back. But I was starting to have doubts. I was no Zen master. This pot had not been given to me. I had stolen it.

"Am I doing the right thing?" I whispered.

The jar told me nothing. For all the significance I attach to artifacts, they are notoriously silent.

Something made a noise down the canyon, an animal moving through brush. I set down the jar, flicked off my lamp. It was an animal of size, a black bear or mountain lion coming to drink from a rock pool a hundred yards away. I stared into the dark, my skin cold. I tucked the pot back into my pack and returned to my sleeping bag. The animal must have smelled our camp or heard me, because it did not come any closer. I lay awake, unable to sleep as I watched stars arc between canyon rims.

. . .

Remarkably, the tide has been slowly turning. Native groups have been increasingly seeing repatriations from institutions around the world. The federal Native American Graves Protection and Repatriation Act of 1990 (NAGPRA) has required the return of the dead and the funerary objects dug up with them, which is a major feat, considering that the Smithsonian alone had been holding the remains of about eighteen thousand individuals.

It feels like trying to pick up after a war while the war is still ongoing, the digging still happening. Many tribes are facing complications because they have no ceremonial framework for returning the dead and their many offerings to the ground. Few had considered it even possible. Who could think of their past being dug up and then slowly regurgitated back into their laps? It is a messy process, one of unexpected transgressions.

When, in 1995, a group of Hopi working on formal repatriations visited the Peabody Museum in Cambridge, they noticed in the card catalog a reference to poisons used on artifacts. As a regular preservation technique, museums had used an assortment of particularly volatile toxins to saturate perishable items in order to prevent decay. It was frequent practice up until the final quarter of the twentieth century, and nobody thought much about it even as NAG-PRA was going into effect and tribes were getting these objects back. Kachinas and other small items were already being sent back to the reservation in Arizona and had been reintroduced into ceremonies, handled by the elderly and by children. Meanwhile, museum guidelines clearly warn, "Unless you can confirm that an object is safe, handle all museum objects as though they were treated with a toxic compound." But nobody had told the Hopi their ceremonial objects had been poisoned. How do you even say something like that?

The ones that had gone back were tested as soon as the problem was revealed. They showed dangerous levels of arsenic and mercury. Artifacts repatriated to another tribe then came up with unhealthy levels of DDT and PDB (fumigants for killing fabric pests), naphthalene (mothballs), and lindane (neurotoxic insecticide). A tribe from New York decided to check fifty-seven medicine masks, and found all were contaminated with arsenic.

Tests continued, and other tribes began finding their objects impregnated with ethylene oxide (which can cause seizure, coma, lungs filling with fluid), methyl bromide (which can cause headaches, dizziness, nausea, vomiting, convulsions), and sulfuryl fluoride (which can cause respiratory irritation and neurological symptoms). When the Elam in northern California found thirty items laced with such concoctions, a tribal leader said, "When our dance regalia are worn out, our tradition is to send them back into the water. If they're toxic, how are we ever going to get rid of them?"

It is alarming to open a drawer in a museum looking for ceremonial objects such as feathered rattles and woven sashes, and find them sealed inside plastic bags with bright red warning labels reading POISON. The irony is that nobody meant any harm by doing this; these preservation techniques

were done by the book. In trying to preserve sacred artifacts, museums perverted them into death carriers. Trying
to do the right thing and to follow the law, they then gave
them back. Mistakes pile on mistakes. We often do not even
know what we have done until much later. How many
wrongs could it possibly take to make a right?

As I traveled with this jar in my pack, I could not help
imagining the mistake embedded in my action, perhaps a
researcher in the future finding the display case and bemoan-
ing the one missing pot, a key to some unforeseeable mystery. I had broken a whole grave assemblage. Wherever I left
the vessel, it would say a hell of a lot more about me and my
ideal than it would about the lives of the people who made
it. As Cornelius Holtorf, a radical and forward-thinking
archaeologist at the University of Lund, in Sweden, put it,
archaeology is significant "not because it manages to import
actual past relics into the present but because it allows us to
recruit past people and what they left behind for a range of
contemporary human interests, needs, and desires." I was
putting this jar back to push against the flood, which means
I was recruiting it for my own desires. I had made myself
another player in the artifact wars. Good intentions or not, I
now felt like a looter.

I tried to shake these thoughts from my head, focus on
navigating my feet through shadowy fields of boulders, but
they stayed with me. Once the artifact is out of the ground,
it's pretty much nothing but trouble.

Already on this journey I had fallen and broken two fingers on my right hand and splinted them with dirty ban-
dages. After that I had taken a harder fall when my boot
slipped and I tumbled, popping three ribs on the side of a
boulder, the dislocation making the sound of a gunshot in
my head as I hit the ground. I cut a strip of fabric and tied it
around my chest, wincing to breathe. Usually I am not so

clumsy. Walking canyons like this since childhood, I had never before broken a bone. Maybe it was this monkey on my back, this jar messing with my head.

I had made a thief of myself, and my moral compass was spinning. Before this I had come to treat archaeology delicately. I strived to be a ghost. But now I had stepped into a trap, a double bind. I had made a new mistake to correct an old one. Welcome to the ethical morass of archaeology and repatriation.

Years later I spoke about these issues with an archaeologist, a Navajo man named Will Tsosie from Arizona.

"My upbringing and my culture say we only let go once, only put people away once, and hope no one will disturb them," Tsosie said. "We hope they will slowly return to the earth. The objects we study are also in the process of returning. Everything lives, everything has a spirit—grass, rock, vessel—and at some point they turn back."

Tsosie told me that once while visiting a museum, he noticed Navajo ceremonial masks on display, and they struck him as very out of place. He said, "It was just like when my father was young, when he was part of a relocation program to get jobs in cities. He got shipped off to Chicago, where he went to the Field Museum, and there he saw the same thing. He spoke to the masks, asking them, 'Why are you here?' saying, 'You don't belong here.' I didn't know it then, about him, but I did the same thing. I said to the masks, 'What are you doing here? You probably miss the voices, you miss the songs, you miss the landscape. You should go home.' It made me very sad. People don't realize that certain things have power. They have spirit. They need to go back."

I explained to Tsosie that I once returned a jar to the wilderness, and he laughed, a bit uncomfortable with my confession. Was I a hero for what I had done or a fool? I did not dare ask him.

Peering up a ravine in the midafternoon, we could make out wood beams high over our heads, hints of a ruin. Dumping our packs, we went up one after the next, picking our way along a steep chute. It was not a death-defying climb, just hard, exactly what the original builders had in mind when they chose the spot. It was a small outpost, a turret inside the canyon. The structure was made of stone and mud, walls half dumped in on themselves. It had just enough purchase on the cliff to maintain a one-story building the color of the rock behind it, its entryway painstakingly engineered into a number of small interior rooms. We ducked in.

Pothunters had been here. Graves lay upended around us. By the looks of things, the pothunters had camped here for a night or two. Off in the corner was a cache of their garbage, fish tins and glass bottles. I picked up a Texsun grapefruit juice can punched with two triangular holes. They had been here in the 1960s. If they had left candy bar wrappers and twist ties dating back a few years, I would have considered it trash, fisted it all into my pack and hauled it out of here. But a Texsun can with its brittle paper label was just a bit older, its story stretching almost a generation out of my reach. That made it worth something: not a full-blown artifact in my mind, but not entirely rubbish. I set it back in the bed it had made for itself over the past few decades. It was now telling the story of pothunters, another layer of history in this ruin.

There is no getting around the fact that age gives objects value. What is your high school yearbook worth? Right now, next to nothing. But bury it in a vault, then dig it up in a few centuries, and it will be precious, a tangible, almost private record of the past. Keep it for a few thousand years and it will be priceless. Why? Rarity and time. Year by year our possessions vanish. We lose the bows and arrows, the buffalo coins, the rotary telephones. Only a select, sometimes accidental few make it through the breach, and those few take on meaning from the stories they carry.

Even the pothunters who had been here were a piece of history in themselves. They were probably like me: adventure-seeking archaeology nuts, the sixties version. Back then, you could hardly sell a pot for more than $25. Digging would have been motivated by raw curiosity more than anything.

This was not the place to leave the jar. Modern diggers would reach this ruin soon enough, screening out the old spoil piles, picking up whatever the sixties pothunters had missed. In a modern market where artifacts from around here go for thousands or tens of thousands of dollars, the game has changed. I wanted to put the jar someplace where no one would see it for many years, maybe centuries, maybe never, make it part of the landscape and take it out of the loop of ownership.

. . .

I had no documentation to tell me where exactly the jar had been unearthed. Putting it "back" was my own notion. I could get it close to the original spot at least, adding a bit of color to the land. We traveled in a canyon bottom, a sinuous cut through solid stone not designed for human movement. Everything was large, boulders the size of elephants, steps too big for stepping. Coming to a twenty-foot plunge, the other two threw their packs over the edge, let them sail and land with a cavernous *humph* on the gravel below. My pack was handled differently. We set up a rope, sent a climber down, and lowered it into outstretched hands.

These canyon bottoms were wearing us thin, a hard way

of travel. It was feeling more and more like trespass every day. I did not want to be seen by anyone. How would I possibly explain my cargo? Usually on reservations I would run into someone on horseback, or sit with an old man in his hogan drinking coffee, discussing options for foot travel. Usually they would tell me allowable routes to follow. This time I made sure we did not meet anyone: we were going on instinct into the shadowy interior. This made for challenging travel—roping packs through gorges, climbing hand over foot.

We decided to go up in elevation, put a few miles under our belts in higher country, maybe find some ruins to explore up there. We just wanted a break from what was so far about sixty miles of dogged travel. We climbed through a side canyon into sunlight, and there we saw him, a man silhouetted against the sky about five hundred feet above us. With a .22 rifle slung on his shoulder and another guy standing near him, he looked like he was out hunting. We must have made an impression, three travelers wearing behemoth packs springing up in the middle of nowhere. When we gave a friendly wave he pulled the rifle and with one hand hoisted it over his head. He looked like a beacon, the classic Apache pose. We stared at him for a moment. Seeing that we did not get his point, he sighted his rifle and popped a few bullets into the boulders above us.

We got the message, darting like deer down the nearest exit. We clambered over ledges and across fallen debris. He kept shooting behind us, aiming at the sky for all we knew, fastening the locks on a door we were not supposed to open. We had permission to be here, a stamp from the tribal council, but paper is not worth much in the reservation interior. He did not want us dead. He just wanted us gone. We obliged, returning to the depths.

The shooting revived us. Springing on each other's heels,

we flew down into a deepening gorge. At the hard stone floor we jogged to a halt. Panting, we glanced at one another.

A nervous laugh.

"What was that?"

"A hunter."

"He didn't want us here."

"He might have had better aim if he knew what was in your pack."

. . .

That night we slept just below a crumble-faced cliff dwelling, the one spot flat enough to camp in a thicket of boulders and mountain mahogany bushes. Again I was awake in my bag until late, my head tilted back so I could see darker shadows inside the upside-down ruin. People have told me they hear drums in canyons like these, something out of the past. I never have, but I do not doubt we each hear something different. I tried not to think of ghosts, just pleasant thoughts, appreciating the richness of stars overhead. But I kept staring at the ruin. I felt like a kid under his covers fixated on a closet door.

I imagined Salado graves in the ground beneath me, skeletons not yet dug, grave offerings in situ. It changes a place to know that it still has physical ancestry, its most vivid human recollection more that just shovel marks and Texsun cans. Even if you don't see it on the surface, you feel the oldness in the ground, artifacts buried and untouched. I thought that if there were such things as ghosts, I was stirring them by passing through here with this jar, as if moving through a curling fog.

In the morning we swept up our gear, brushed away the marks of our sleeping, and left. This was far enough. One more day of walking beyond the pothunted ruin and past the man with the rifle had brought us through miles of twists and turns. This was the right terrain for leaving the jar: plenty of cliffs and hiding places, and deep enough into the reservation to weed out most casual travelers.

We took a side canyon back to a hollow space where the land boxed itself in. We ditched our packs and carried the jar by hand. We spotted a niche in the rock and climbed to it, passing the vessel from one person to the next. The space was free of dust, out of the weather, and practically invisible, a slender-shadowed aerie in the rock. I intended this vessel to outlast the hardiest searchers, its craft glue and masking tape slowly dissolving, the jar eventually falling in two in the land where it was made.

I held it for one last moment, sorry to see it leave and glad all the same. Then I reached the jar into its shelter and left it there. I had no words prepared, no ceremony, had never done anything like it before and was damn sure I would not do anything like it again. Robin Hood, my ass. I felt I was making more of a mess out of an already intractable situation. By picking it up and bringing it here, I had claimed the jar as my own. The only thing this theft-and-return stunt did was make me more uncertain of how to strike a balance.

CHAPTER 3

TREASURE HUNTERS

It is our hands. They want to touch everything. With fingers like these, the kind that turn pages and pick up the head of a pin, how could we ever call them off?

It is our bodies, our eyes, the rivers of senses. We relate to the world physically. The rest is just talk.

A man, a registered nurse from Phoenix named Robert Schroeder, wanted to see a boulder in Arizona so heavily embellished with rock art it is known as Newspaper Rock (one of many in the Southwest). This one, though, is off limits because over the years visitors have damaged it. Too much touching. Now you can approach it on a trail and look over a railing (a spotting scope helps for detail), but Schroeder wanted to get closer.

He and his girlfriend left home in the dark on a Christmas morning, figuring no one would be there. He parked his car at an inconspicuous location and walked in. Along the way, they found many boulders covered with rock art, more than he had ever imagined. He was jubilant. He took note of patterns of sand frozen in a wash along the way and marveled at how it snowed that day, his first white Christmas ever. It was one of the most magical days of his life. At least it was until he ran into two federal rangers with sniper rifles and a bullhorn. He had not realized there were motion sensors they had tripped.

Schroeder and his terrified girlfriend hid behind dry brush, which only made matters worse, while the rangers waited them out. Soon enough they were handcuffed, and his camera was confiscated. He was embarrassed and angry. He certainly knew he was doing something illegal—thus the hiding—but he felt that with earnest effort and a delicate touch, one should have the right to visit a rock art–covered boulder. He said he saw so much rock art that morning, it was a testament to the people who lived here. What most visitors see beyond the railing is one boulder marked up with images. They don't realize the much larger context, the entire landscape an ancient book. His cost: apprehension and fines.

Schroeder told me, "When one looks at pictures of petroglyphs, say in a book or on a computer, they simply become aware of them. But to stand in front of one, to see it up close and realize the amount of skill and effort and time it took to make it, that's when one appreciates the petroglyph as opposed to simply being aware of it."

One wonders how to balance our deeds. How vivid must our appreciation be? How close do we need to get? A site meant to connect people with the past by means of informative displays and closed-off areas gives a picture of a lonely petroglyph-covered boulder when it is actually one of hundreds. But allowing greater access goes far beyond budgeting for parking pullouts, trails, law enforcement, and conservation. Humans being what we are, rock saws would come out and people would start carrying pieces home.

I have paused in museums at ancient religious sculptures with their lips and feet worn away from centuries of being kissed and knew that if I leaned too close, an alarm would sound or a guard would stop me, and for good reason. We would kiss these things out of existence. There are so many of us now that we threaten to devour the world with all our touching, starting with the things we adore most. At the same time, we obviously yearn for contact, and I fear what would happen if we were cut off from a distinctive, on-the-ground relationship with the past.

. . .

I belong to a gang of relic hunters. For one solid decade we spent seasons scouring the wilderness, climbing in and out of every piece of ground before us, lowering and raising our gear on ropes. We were looking for unaltered archaeology, sites still crisp after centuries or thousands of years of quiescence. No railings, no trails, no signs, no glass. That is the treasure we were after. If Schroeder had been with us, he would have seen plenty of rock art. But we were after portable artifacts more than anything: baskets, pots, and sandals left behind, precious belongings that people cared for, then cached away. Mostly we found clean desert boulders and many long months of walking. We touched so much of the country, at times our fingerprints wore clean off. Part of it was the rush of discovery, the surprise of a sugar-white spearhead or a thatched cradleboard half submerged in dust. It was about being human, moving like a human, finding what humans left behind. You would come to a place to sit and rest, and then realize someone else had done the same a thousand years earlier, knapping an arrowhead and leaving a ring of flaked stone at your feet. Then you would glance around, looking down corridors of horizon and at the shape of the sky, your body taking the perfect place of someone long ago, as if you were the shadow. That is the kind of privilege we were after.

We did our best to leave hardly a footprint, priding ourselves as sort of cat burglars of the desert, the kind of people who would break into your house, look in your medicine cabinet, uncap the spices in your kitchen to smell each one and put them back. No one would ever know we were here, nothing taken or out of place. There was one time we moved an artifact—a ninth-century ceramic canteen—and two days later buried it twenty feet away in hopes that no one would steal it. But even that felt awkward. I returned some years later to put the small round jar back, tipping it under the shadow of a rock outcrop just the way we had found it, as if putting the moon back in the sky. I wanted it there because it was what Schroeder had risked his freedom to see: a thing just as it had been for all those years.

One late autumn a few of us were trekking through the banded red-and-white sandstones of southeast Utah. My wife, Regan, had split off one morning to explore for ruins. She was five months pregnant, just beginning to show, and she said she wanted some time alone. We said we would meet back up in a few days, and I left with Dirk, a former street cop gone wilderness, a midforties Hayduke. Dirk and I knew each other's moves as if we were twin monkeys leaping and crawling through this stony wonderland.

"We're looking for a wrinkle in the land," said Dirk when we stopped for lunch, his back leaning against a rock, a rubber-gripped knife unfolded on his knee for whittling a hard block of cheese. "Something out of place, a notch or a crack, just enough to catch the eye."

He cast his voice from our balcony of rock jutting hundreds of feet above a canyon floor. The region had already been picked over by other artifact hunters, cleaned like roadkill. But even here we found routes that looked untouched, and ruins left to their own decay. We were constantly searching for the keys to these inner houses. When we stopped talking, we listened to the stiff sound of wind through bristling ephedra bushes.

We closed up lunch, and I hoisted my pack onto my shoulders, dodging around a crooked boulder to start up a route to the canyon rim. Dipping my head I noticed an arc of shade beneath the boulder five feet from where we had been sitting. I dropped another inch, just enough to see the outside curve of a jar beside a stone metate. The jar was half buried in a drift of sand. The metate, an old grinding stone, was placed beside it, and they looked as orderly as a fork and spoon on a table.

"Bingo," I said and fell to my knees. "It's a pot."

"The hell you say," Dirk said.

A smile filled my face as I looked at a delicate seed jar with blow-sand up around its side, its mouth a willing little O aiming into the air. "It's right here."

Dirk was immediately beside me kneeling in red dust. I had my pack half off, crooked on my back, too amazed to finish my business.

"No shit, there it is," Dirk said.

Like the barbarians we were, Dirk and I locked forearms, grinning wildly. It takes years to come across something like this, a perfect jar beaming before us.

The sting of discovery slowly settled. I did not pay much attention to the metate. I had seen plenty of metates. It was the jar that had me, an early type known as Deadman's Black-on-Red. It had a broad hip and a restricted entry, one that would allow only your fingers to scoop seeds. This design dates back to the very beginning of pottery in North America. In local excavations, seed jars like these are generally found one per household. They were family heirlooms passed generation to generation. Thinking back to my own household, my father even left me a seed jar when he died, a rare Pueblo piece made by Acoma potter Lucy Lewis that now sits on my desk and collects sewing needles. Even Regan came to our marriage with her own seed jar, a red narrow-mouthed vase from her Korean grandmother. If not a jar, it might be a favorite platter or a polished jewelry box handed down. It is what you grab when your house is burning.

I could see it happening here a thousand years ago, a village emptied on the mesa top, people moving away with whatever they could carry. It was a time of intertribal warfare and migration, some settlements abandoned gradually, others burning as people ran. What could not be carried was either left for pillage or hidden in the canyons.

One side of the jar and the entire lower half were buried. Dirk used his fingertips to delicately flick sand away, just enough to reveal the extent of black paint scrolled around its mouth. Doing this, he exposed a tiny crack, and then two small drill holes to either side of it. A tight, weathered braid of yucca fibers had been laced through both holes. It was a repair job. The crack had formed while the jar was still in use, and its owners had drilled holes (probably with a bone awl), then cinched the crack tight. They had cared for this jar. It had been loved.

Time squeezed tighter for me. Rings between years touched until they became almost transparent as I saw a hand guiding these artifacts under this boulder, sliding them out of sight. I did not want the setting changed. After taking a pot to put it back, I was not so comfortable with inserting myself freely into the much longer life of any other artifact. I preferred to back away, nothing altered, no one notified. We were never here. No longer would I open any shrine.

Unexpectedly, Dirk said he wanted this one moved, "just far enough that we can protect it." We had noticed hairline cracks, which would eventually cause the jar to come apart like a dead flower, ceramic petals dropping in the dust.

"Look here, there's a drip that lands on it," Dirk said. He traced a finger to the jar's backside where maybe five or ten drops of rainwater got in every year, wearing away a hole.

He said we could give it another several hundred years of life if we got it to better shelter.

I countered, "What, we hide it someplace else so that nobody will see it for another eight hundred years? Why not leave it where it is? At least let it die here."

I liked the clutter of the land and the pathways secreted inside it containing pinpoints of human memory. I liked the way the jar was sitting here, telling its small story to no one for all this time. And now Dirk wanted the story changed.

He said I was being a sentimental pansy.

He was right, but I saw it first, so it was my call to make. Finders keepers. I told him it was staying. Disappointed, Dirk said he was at least going to cover it with a rock so it would not be seen by anyone else, thus preventing it from being stolen. He came back and fitted a plate of sandstone into place, but it looked terrible, just what I'd expect from someone trying to hide something. It felt like a railing. Dirk's inner cop, the guy with the bullhorn and sniper rifle, was coming out. He did not want any unscrupulous soul touching this jar.

"Get that out of there," I said.

"It needs something," he objected.

"It doesn't need anything, Dirk," I said. "It's been here for eight hundred goddamned years!"

The curator in me agreed with Dirk, while the fatalist happily watched this jar sink into oblivion. We didn't solve our problem right there. It was late in the day at that point, and we agreed to come back in the morning. We backtracked into the next canyon before nightfall and found Regan. She appeared a few hundred feet above us, her head poking over the red bulb of a cliff near where she was camped. We shouted up to her that we had found something beautiful that she must see.

Like a Neolithic Romeo I called to her, "Meet tomorrow in the notch between canyons!"

With cracked lips, she blew a kiss.

The next morning we found each other. Dirk and I took Regan to the boulder, where she paused before noticing the jar and gave a great smile. Waddling slightly from pregnancy, she dropped her pack, hoisted up her belt loops, and squatted. She went down on her knees, then elbows as she crawled beneath the boulder, running her eye along the jar's rim. For a good ten minutes she remained down there, face to face, admiring our discovery with soft, diagnostic words.

She hauled herself out, wiped off her hands, and said, "Did you guys notice it's shattered?"

"We saw the cracks," we said.

"But did you see it's completely come apart?" she repeated. "The only thing holding it together is the sand."

Dirk and I knelt down for a closer look. She was right. The jar had already fallen apart but was packed in place by what the wind had blown in. If we had tried to move it, it would have crumbled in our hands like our own breaking hearts. We would have destroyed it.

I told Dirk, "See."

Dirk still wanted it saved. He found a new rock to wedge into place, blocking the view. He complained, "Some monkey's going to come along and take it."

"So?" I asked.

Dirk snorted, weary of my whimsical liberalism.

Regan let us go on for a few rounds. Then she said flatly, "You guys need to stop arguing and leave the thing alone."

We looked up at her. She was serious, and you do not deny a pregnant woman anything, especially on your knees before her. The jar was not ours. It belonged to someone who died long ago, who put it here so that no one else would take it. We got what we came for, evidence of the past that we could get up close to and surround with our senses. Our job here was done. We did as Regan said, packed up and followed her out of there, Dirk's rock dropped to the side, a mark of dispute now part of the story. Like those before us, we never returned.

~~~~~~~~~~~~~~~

CHAPTER 4

UNSEEN THINGS

L ong ago people lived on the eroded surface of a region known today as the Four Corners, their horizons studded by abrupt rock towers and faraway blue mountains. The people now have many names, for no one recalls what they might have called themselves. The Hopi have one word for them, Navajos another, archaeologists yet another: Hisatsinom, Anasazi, Ancestral Puebloan. Around the tenth century, these people went from smaller sites and scattered hamlets to constructing monumental architecture, ceremonial features up to five stories tall that took up acres on the ground. They were domesticating animals, relying heavily on agricultural surplus, and were not far from early metallurgy.

Based on the languages of their living descendants, it seems that at least seven different tongues were spoken among the people. Some had completely different roots, which implies that they came from distant places to make a cohesive prehistoric culture. In this dry and formidable landscape the people once numbered around 20,000, near carrying capacity for the marginal growing climate of the Four Corners. Some years they produced an abundance of corn, squash, pumpkins, beans, and amaranth. In other years they nearly starved.

They made beautiful ceramics, pendants, fetishes, and loom-woven textiles — millions of objects that now fill shops and decorate museums and private collections around the world.

The teeth of these people have been found worn down and glassy due to the amount of sand in their diets, the result of frequent dust storms and the ubiquity of sand across the entire region. Since life expectancy was tied directly to dental health, the average person lived only to around thirty. When their teeth were gone, they were dead.

Those who died either went into the ground or were scattered upon it, and those who were buried usually went with an array of offerings: jars, mugs, weaving tools, weapons, and jewelry.

Their presence in the Four Corners was abruptly truncated late in the twelfth century. The reason: increased population, a debilitating drought, violent social upheaval, and a penchant for cultural mobility. Within a period of ten years all construction stopped throughout the region, and the people were gone. Most left for other lands in the south, where they became the modern Pueblo tribes. In the walls of the kivas they left behind were ritual items. In shrines on hilltops and in caves they planted centuries of offerings. The apparatus of an upstart civilization became buried in red sand, the very sand that had blown into their mouths, weathering them back into the ground.

This is how an archaeological record is formed.

What you do or don't do with it from there is well worth considering.

. . .

There was a woman named Susan, a senior writer for the *Los Angeles Times*. She wanted to do a story on the way we traveled in this storied landscape. A few of us were heading south from Utah into Arizona. We told her to come find us at a resupply, a grocery store in Blanding, Utah, where we arrived wild and unshowered. Susan showed up in tennis shoes and a backpack. She had a sleeping bag, a jacket, a notebook. Other necessary equipment we loaned her out of our own gear.

Heading west along the rutted back roads of Cedar Mesa, we gave her a crash course in detecting archaeology. Carrying backpacks, we dropped off-trail, leading her along canyon edges and down boulder-choked routes to find potsherds and stone flakes, showing her how you can follow scattered pieces to their source and locate a settlement or prehistoric work area, hunting blind, or ambush spot. As soon as she found her first piece of pottery with her own eyes, she could barely look up from the ground. She could hardly walk ten feet without bending down to pick up something, see what it is.

Middle-aged, smart, and well traveled, Susan could have made us look ridiculous in print, and she once commented that it was as if we were Lost Boys exploring Never Never Land. Yet she was also gripped by the magnificence of the terrain and the possibility of discovery. Yes, we were a band of smelly yahoos, but we had a point. You start getting an eye, and the land opens up. If you had such a skill, would you not wander through the world peering at the history beneath your feet?

In the morning, we climbed through the layers of a canyon and entered a spacious natural alcove. A small thirteenth-century household had been built here, masonry footers and the hatchwork of wattle-and-daub construction half standing. On the floor was the carnage of a fresh and precise dig. A pothunter had been here only a few months before us and made a hole in the center of the floor. Pueblo ancestors one or two thousand years ago had dug out an underground chamber, put something in it, and capped it with an adobe plug the size of a dinner plate. The cap was broken to pieces and discarded. Inside there had been a den of soft juniper bark used as packaging material. I lowered my head into the hole and saw about ten gallons of empty space patted down with plaster to keep out moisture and rodents. The digger had pulled out the bark hand over hand and tossed it aside like a kid tearing wrapping paper off a present. What had he found?

It could have been the mummy of an infant still in its cradleboard. Or maybe it was a loom-woven blanket, a clutch of polished fetishes, a feathered headdress. Whatever it was, the original owners had swaddled it carefully and packed it away, and now it was gone.

I moved over, gave Susan room to look inside.

I said, "Most of them got dug out a long time ago. I'm surprised this one lasted so long."

"What was in here?" she asked.

Dirk, crouching at the hole. "Something important. Something they wanted safe."

"Who did it?" Susan asked.

"A pothunter," I said. "Maybe somebody stumbled on it by accident."

"Like one of us?"

Dirk, knowing he was being quoted, rose and said, "We're not diggers." He explained his ethic, saying that we might push away a skim of sand, but we don't go deeper than that. Deeper makes you a digger. She asked what was wrong with digging, and Dirk answered that some things in the world should just be left unseen. We don't have to dig up every last thing. He said that artifacts out here are messages. Finding what past cultures left behind is as close as we can get to meeting the minds of the ancients. But you're respectful of them. You wouldn't go into a graveyard and start digging. That's what this whole place is, a giant graveyard.

Looking at the mess of juniper bark, I thought of stuffing

it back inside, then covering it with handfuls of adobe to at least clean up the mess, but putting it back empty would have felt like a parody, a shell game. You don't just toss the lid back on the box, hoping to shut off its emptiness.

The rest of us poked around the space, finding broken adobe footers of old rooms and granaries, while Susan remained standing at the hole looking inside like a girl peering down a well, her imagination flying. When we left we had to call her away.

.   .   .

Early one afternoon Susan and I lost the others in our party. Each drifted away to his or her own discoveries, while the two of us explored the sun-bright south face of a canyon. We shed our coats, tucked them in daypacks. Susan pulled out her notebook and asked me questions about why my companions and I travel so relentlessly, what drives us to look in every crack for the hope of some old thing. I told her it was the same reason she couldn't look up after her first potsherd. We're infected.

A row of stout cliff dwellings appeared around the bend, little buildings mortared into fissures a few hundred feet above the canyon bottom. They were sturdy dwellings, with doors you could barely fit through. I urged Susan not to try the narrower doors, explaining that those rooms are closed, too easy to brush against the wood and plaster, over time wearing out the structure's integrity. I showed her to a wider entrance, and we ducked inside to find a low ceiling of soot-black wood beams riddled with fresh corks. Each cork had a catalogue number. Susan touched them, puzzled. Archaeologists had been here. They had taken core samples, dating the wood down to the very season it was cut. To fill the holes, they pounded corks into place and smoothed them flush to the wood.

This was a known site, its floors smooth from traffic, maybe a few hundred people a year. There is no law against exploring sites like this as long as you are careful. You take off your pack so you don't accidentally brush against a wall, and you move slowly through the dark, rectangular entryways without touching their wooden lintels or smooth adobe jambs. I have learned over the years just to go barefoot. Susan and I drifted apart through the rooms, until I found her several minutes later sitting on a floor in a dim space where wood rats had been living for centuries. It was a blocky room, with a ceiling about four feet high. Daylight reduced to bare shade around her. I could see her face, the red of sandstone reflected in her cheeks. She was sifting her hand through blow-sand, little pills of wood-rat droppings slipping between her fingers. I sat down with her. There was just enough space that we were touching slightly, a comfort that comes between people after a few days in the wilderness. As she greeted me, her hand kept moving through the dusty floor. She sent her fingers a little deeper each time, as if looking for a toy in a sandbox. I was about to remind her that if she was thinking about digging she should stop, but she hit something hard. I stared as she began sweeping away dirt, exposing a flat, round stone. It was flush to a plastered floor.

She tapped on the stone, put her ear to it.

"Hollow," she said.

I could hear it, too. There was a space beneath.

"What is it?" she asked.

"Looks like a doorstone," I said, surprised. Given the number of people who had probably visited this room, it seemed unlikely they had missed anything. Maybe they forgot to look, assumed everything was taken.

"Doorstone?"

"A hatch, like the adobe plug that guy pulled up."

She nodded and kept brushing sand away. I felt suspended in disbelief, as if gravity were beginning to fail. How could this be?

She ran a finger around the outline of the stone, pressing the dust to reveal a mortar seal, while I tried not to let my mind flood down beneath her, tried not to go shoulder to shoulder with Susan and say, *By God, you found something important, not bad for a beginner.*

I did not want to say anything that would cloud this moment for her. She was the one who had found it, not me.

"Come on, you have all the answers, what do you think it is?" she asked.

"Artifacts," I said. "Whatever that guy was looking for in the juniper bark."

"They're still here?"

"Probably."

She traced the stone again with her finger, making its shape clearer, and said, "Would you tell anybody about it?"

"You mean archaeologists?"

"Yeah."

"No. I never do," I said. "Most of the ones I know don't want to hear about it. They'd have to make an assessment and probably remove the contents so they wouldn't get stolen. The ones I know are tired of that game."

I could not help watching Susan's hands, begging her in my mind to cover this back over and leave it alone. Yet I wanted her to open the space, to pry back the stone and show me its contents. My heart was starting to beat too fast, and I was afraid she could see it through my shirt.

Whatever lay beneath was offering itself to her, but she was just a tourist, someone passing through. Could all these centuries possibly lead only to her?

"You could just get your fingers under it and open it," she said.

"You could," I replied.

"What should I do?"

"What do you want to do?"

"Come on, you've been in this situation before. What should I do?"

I shook my head. Having once uncapped a small rock pyramid to see what was inside, I had no right to stop her.

She let out a frustrated breath.

I did not want to force my own ethic on her. I had done it before, only to find later that people had defiantly pocketed a pretty potsherd or a wooden bow I had beseeched them not to take. As she kept asking me what to do, the room began to feel smaller. I wanted out. At the same time, I wanted to help her get that stone off. Our craving is what reveals itself in places like this. I have worked at archaeological digs, museum and university projects where crews are on hands and knees slowly scraping out the past by eighth-inch increments as if in a barely controlled mania, and I often feel that if given permission, we would tear the ground apart with shovels and picks in a frenzy to find what is in there. There are truly treasures down inside, keys to the past, ways of seeing an older world. We want to be the first ones to bridge the gap, clearing the dust away and letting in light. But if we opened it, the seal would be broken. It would be forever changed. It would be ours.

There is a difference between finding and keeping. The two are often lumped together into one action, but there is a blink that comes in between. It is when a thing goes from being its own to being yours. It happened when archaeologist Howard Carter used hot knives to cut off King Tutankhamen's amulets and mask, which had hardened into the mummy's resin. It was when he severed the arms and legs of the dead king, split the torso in two, and cut off the head—just to make transporting easier. That part is the taking, when you claim ownership. King Tutankhamen now looks resplendent and vulnerable, both his golden mask and the charcoal-colored ball of his head on traveling display, but resplendent and vulnerable are not what Carter originally witnessed. He saw time cracking open, the shadow of every hand still there in the tomb, poised where each let go of a burial good. When he first broke into the chamber, Carter had peered inside the nimbus of his candlelight, and when someone beside him asked what was in there, Carter replied famously, breathlessly, "Wonderful things."

An archaeologist named Glade Hadden once told me, "For me, the thrill of discovery is the juice. I get that juice once with each artifact I find. If I take it with me, it doesn't add to the thrill of the finding, and if I leave it there it doesn't take away from the thrill of finding. It does, however, give someone else the possibility of the same joy of finding. And, truthfully? I feel better about myself when I leave it behind. Maybe some perverse form of ego reinforcement, but hey— it works, it leaves things intact, something that's becoming more and more rare."

Susan was not talking about taking anything, but as far as I was concerned the mere act of opening the hatch would break the spell, another mystery cracked.

I got up off my knees. I wanted no part of this decision. It was her discovery, not mine.

"I'll be outside," I said. "Brush out your tracks when you leave."

I walked into the hot midday shine of adobe knowing what Susan would decide, at least hoping I did. When I was far enough away I stopped and looked out over the canyon, clearing my mind.

. . .

We have no single agreed-upon way of treating the past. Behavior varies from person to person. I recall a Polaroid of a pothunter holding up a freshly unearthed human skull and sticking his tongue into its mouth, an act of grotesquely ultimate possession. Where do right and wrong come into play? Where do you draw the line, and is there any way an agreement can broadly be met on that line? Most of us can agree you don't French-kiss a skull. Yet, what do you do with scrabbling curiosity and a sealed hatch on the floor? To open it would break centuries of cultural stasis, damaging a sensitive site. Leaving it closed is like biting your tongue until it bleeds.

I would have prevented Susan from digging, or putting something in her pocket to take home, but I could not dictate what she should do with that stone.

Many archaeologists say that the magnitude of archaeological destruction requires an ironclad ethic, and in the absence of that, harsher laws. They will tell you that every specimen is important. We do not have access to half of our physical history because half (or far more) of the archaeological record has been destroyed, and what has gone into private hands generally lacks the documentation that would define any artifact's position in the ground. Without a three-dimensional picture of where an artifact is from, it is lost to science. But the dictates of science are not the only reason.

The quality so often sought among ancient objects is their being untouched, previously unseen, no modern liberties taken that would muddy their ties to the past. Once we get our hands on them, we change them, make them part of our time. There comes a point when it is of greater value to leave things unchanged, not for science but for the things themselves.

When Susan finally emerged from the room, she stepped up beside me, a hundred layers of horizon before us, a squat row of cliff dwellings and their dark openings at our backs. She had left the doorstone sealed, and she seemed a bit miffed not to have seen what was inside, and annoyed that I had left her. Or maybe she was just perplexed at this whole situation. Either way, I could finally breathe easier.

PART TWO

VANDALISM AND OTHER ACTS
OF REMOVAL

~~~~~~~~~~~~~~~

CHAPTER 5

DIGGERS

The gray-green wind-sweep of St. Lawrence Island in the Bering Strait is one of the few remaining nonsubmerged parts of the land bridge that once connected Siberia to North America. It has been occupied for the past 2,000 years, since the rise of Julius Caesar in Rome and the zenith of Teotihuacán in the Valley of Mexico. For thousands of years the island has been populated by whale and walrus hunters, their ancient villages now buried beneath the tundra. A shovel in the right place can break into a nest of carved artifacts: figurines, harpoons, net weights, and fire starters. Parts of the island are practically made of artifacts, smaller pieces selling as novelties from a few dollars apiece to a few hundred. Five hundred or six hundred dollars can buy you a knife with a handle made from an ancient sled runner. Sometimes a rare Okvik idol will appear, a human figurine with arched eyes and a thin, elongated nose, fetching $100,000 or more. In 2006 a pair of fancifully engraved snow goggles carved from walrus tusk and estimated to be a thousand years old sold for $216,000 at Christie's in New York. Wholesale buyers frequently arrive to pick up these raw artifacts, most made from walrus ivory or whalebone, dropping about $1.5 million on the island every year (this breaks down to about $1,000 each for residents). The diggers who supply these buyers are native islanders who speak Siberian Yupik. Unearthing and selling their own ancestry, many say that these are gifts left by ancestors to help them survive in a cash economy.

Politically, the island is part of Alaska. Although the artifacts are being moved through the United States, which has ample antiquities laws, the transactions are legal. The island is owned as a native corporation and is considered private property, which exempts it from most of the laws. Still, there are those who deeply question the ethics. Some locals say that empty holes left in the ground are the cause of social distress and even spiritual debilitation. A far greater outcry has come from archaeologists, who have called St. Lawrence diggers "cultural cannibals," saying they are wantonly selling off their own cultural heritage. They say that when these artifacts are taken without detailed documentation showing strata or pinpoint relationships with surrounding features, the record of people who lived here is permanently damaged. The response from many St. Lawrence Islanders is that they, the living, are what links the past to the present. For them, selling these artifacts continues the tradition of the people who made them, a bloodline of subsistence hunters adapting to changing needs. These people are still very much tied to old lifeways, with half their diet coming from walrus, whale, and seal. Digging artifacts fits easily with seasonal subsistence, as they head to their digging spots in late summer to follow the receding permafrost.

Julie Hollowell, a candid and gentle archaeologist from Princeton, told me that as she was using a trowel on her own excavations on St. Lawrence Island, subsistence diggers would come by and tell her if she didn't get out a good shovel and start seriously digging, she was not going to find anything. Hollowell laughed easily at the exchange. Working on St. Lawrence Island since the mid-1980s, Hollowell has reached across the aisle to talk with native diggers as well as the dealers they work with, while her profession has codified ethics that actively discourage such conversation. She has come to see the islanders not as cultural cannibals but as people with personal reasons as valid as her own for probing the ground. When in 2009 she was involved with an exhibition of St. Lawrence artifacts at a Princeton museum, Hollowell insisted that she would participate only if the museum displayed the full story of how they got there, not just scientific context but the economic issues that brought so many artifacts to the surface in the first place. For her, archaeology includes what is happening now. It does not end when an object becomes buried in the ground.

Hollowell once asked a high school class on the island how many had dug for artifacts, and every hand went up. The people of St. Lawrence are party to the history of these objects. After spending considerable time with them, Hollowell told me she believes these people should be able to make a living from their own material culture. They have a right of ancestry.

How far does that right extend? I know a Navajo pothunter who picks Pueblo Indian pieces off the land and moves them into the market, and though he is deeply possessed by these objects, he is not related to those who made them. His claim is that they are on his reservation, part of the landscape he and several hundred years' worth of his ancestors have occupied. His defense probably would not hold up in court.

Then what about Anglos, descendants of families that have been in the same place for more than a century, each generation going out with shovels to connect with the past in its own way? This goes well beyond James O. Young keeping an arrowhead his mother found in her garden. Many diggers go for prime artifacts regardless of what culture made them. The threads of continuity diminish, tangle, fray, and soon you are far from St. Lawrence Island. The removal of artifacts unravels into chaos, evasion, betrayal, and even death. The place to go for this end of the story is San Juan County, Utah.

. . .

I was crouched, trying to make myself invisible, as an airplane swept in from a desert sky as clear as glass. From under my hat brim I watched a twin-engine Cessna head toward a red-dust hill at my back where a fifty-foot-wide circle marked a buried prehistoric ceremonial house. Nine centuries had collapsed its ceiling, had sent the whole place into the ground with nothing remaining on the surface but a shallow depression strewn with broken pottery. I had found the site only hours earlier, and already it was in someone else's sights.

The plane rushed over my head with a crescendo of propeller roar, and I quickly stood and watched it pass over the hill. It made a sharp upward arc to clear a red palisade beyond it. I was down inside an arrangement of cliffs in a corner of the Navajo reservation, not an easy place to drop a plane into. The pilot was good, though, banking through the summer blue. The noise cut out as the plane slipped behind a butte and returned as the pilot swung around for another approach. For this pass I remained standing, but I still don't think I was spotted. Pilot and passenger were focused on the hilltop, where the buried ruin would have been perfectly visible from above.

It looked as if someone was showing off an investment, money in the ground. Things have come to this: archaeology sold to order. You can look at an untouched mound and put a dollar value on it, say it's going to have at least $10,000 of artifacts inside. This sort of thing happens around the world. A looter in China will show prospective buyers photographs of artifacts in an insufficiently guarded museum, and once a price is agreed upon the objects will be stolen and prepared for transport.

Coming in from the air is easier than on foot. A helicopter had recently been spotted in and out of canyons around here, a bubble-nosed, sunset red Eurocopter (tail number N296SL). It had been seen dipping its tail rotor near the ground and blowing off surface dust to reveal whether there was anything below.

This lower right-hand corner of Utah is an archaeological mecca, one of the richest zones in North America if you want to walk around picking up pots and baskets. Over the past century, with a shovel you could have found anything your heart desired—sandals, skeletons, turquoise ornaments, carved shells. A local pothunter once said that when he found a plain gray pot he would throw it up in the air and chuck a rock at it just to watch it shatter. Considering population estimates and mortality rates, and accounting for several centuries of burial practices, probably half a million graves lie within 25,000 square miles. Upon this terrain you'll find well over 100,000 abandoned, dust-buried settlements ranging in size from once-prosperous pueblos to humble family farmsteads. They leave the earth lumpy and heaved, and in places their fallen timbers stick up like busted telephone poles. I have found evidence of explosives, where old-school pothunters detonated sticks of dynamite under cliff dwellings, blowing them up to more easily access burials underneath. Imagine skeletons tumbling over each other in a disarticulated cascade of pots and turquoise.

It is a race to see who can find the last remaining objects. Anything left in situ is a sitting duck. Land agencies are pulling artifacts from the field, housing them in museums and storage facilities to prevent them being stolen, while pothunters are becoming more sophisticated: lean ones who travel fast and light by foot; belly-fat, gun-heavy ATV folks ramming probes into the ground to find the loose fill of graves; and the in-and-out helicopter types. The highest market value goes to the most serious diggers, those who move quickly from site to site, those backed by investors with their finds sold before they are even discovered. Meth-amphetamine addicts now make up part of the pothunting demographic. Small-town trailer-park labs keep popping up around the Four Corners. In one trailer, agents found a pound and a half of meth (street value a few hundred thou-sand dollars), five loaded firearms, sixteen pounds of mari-juana, and at least thirty to forty intact prehistoric pots. The jittery obsession elicited by meth goes perfectly with run-ning around in the desert looking for artifacts. It is an ideal pastime for people going out of their minds looking for some cash to keep the drugs flowing. But this is not how it started.

.   .   .

People here grew up hunting arrowheads and digging for pots. There was seemingly nothing wrong with it. The law? Hardly anyone even knew the law. For a long time pothunt-ing was not considered a crime around San Juan County. It was more a tradition than a wrongdoing. Even though the country's core antiquities law had been on the books since 1906, it was rarely enforced, a nonentity. A woman who grew up here told me her grandfather would send her to find artifacts just to get her out of his hair.

Sunday picnics in San Juan County often included shov-els and buckets as Mormon families came out to enjoy the canyons and mesas under the clear breadth of the sky. A picnic and some digging, a thermos of coffee, maybe a screen to sift the dirt—what could be wrong with that? There was a time when the country seemed overloaded with abandoned artifacts, when you could not walk without stepping on one. Kids used to rifle through spoil piles for beads or pretty potsherds, while their elders put craters in red soil to make big finds. You used to see human skulls set on the side of the road, hollow eye sockets watching Jeeps and GMCs buzz past. Some diggers sold what they found, but most held on to their prizes, which were worth more as spoils of the hunt. A painted eleventh-century olla in perfect condition granted its discoverer monumental bragging rights in town.

This tradition gained prominence with a little outside help. In the 1920s an archaeologist named Andrew Kerr from the University of Utah in Salt Lake appeared after he heard that an entire quarter of the state was filthy with archaeology right near the surface, graves practically springing from the ground.

Kerr hired local residents to dig; his head diggers were members of the Shumway family, who had already done a good deal of private excavation. The Shumways did most of the work while Kerr sat back. They showed him how to locate the best caches of artifacts, how to dig without breaking pots. Meanwhile, Kerr encouraged them and paid them to become even better at it. Showing little regard for scientific method, he wanted only the most visually stunning artifacts, which he shipped back to the university's museum.

Julie Hollowell once told me a very similar story from back on St. Lawrence Island, where early archaeologists arrived to dig and for the first time impressed locals with the value of what was buried under their feet. She said, "It became obvious to me that the interface with both museum collectors and archaeologists had totally commoditized these objects for them." This phenomenon has been repeated around the world: archaeologists alerting people to the value in the ground, even paying them to find it, starting a momentum that is now difficult to stop.

By the time Kerr was finished in southeast Utah, local residents had gained a taste for relics. When he left, people kept digging to see what else they could find.

Laws against this kind of thing began stacking up in the late 1970s. But members of the Shumway family, among others, stood forth in righteous defense of their God-given right as free Americans to loot and pillage in the tradition of their ancestors. They kept digging.

. . .

Enter Earl Shumway, who made a notorious name for himself as a professional pothunter. He is credited with ruining the tradition by drawing the eye of the law, turning a pastime into a rebel sport. During the height of his digging career in the 1980s and '90s he claimed to have dug 10,000 archaeological sites, turning them into sloppy messes where he left behind calling cards of Mountain Dew cans and cigarette butts (his claim to so many sites has been refuted by those who say he could not have come close to that number, yet there is no doubt that he did his share, even employing bulldozers). Heading into the backcountry well armed, he shared a local Dukes of Hazzard mentality that grew from the Sagebrush Rebellion, a general antifederal atmosphere in the West. Archaeology was a convenient vehicle.

Multiple branches of law enforcement were after him for years. In that vast and mostly empty country he was hard to track or pin down and evidence against him was difficult to gather. Whenever he returned home to the small town of Blanding, he was full of bravado as he romanced reporters on the phone, boasting that he was armed and dangerous and making a handsome and very illegal living off the black market.

Most people who knew Earl well would not talk to me about him (on the record at least). He was said to be mixing drug deals and pothunting, a common merger in the underworld of global antiquities but new to rural southeast Utah. A filmmaker who followed him in the late 1980s called Earl charming as could be, a boisterous storyteller who enjoyed an audience. On the other side of the coin, when he last got out of prison, he publicly stated that he would kill any federal officer he encountered in the backcountry. A ranger who worked the region in the 1990s told me it was because of people like Earl that she wore a bulletproof life vest when running rivers. She carried a SIG Sauer 9-mm sidearm with forty rounds on her person, kept on hand a 12-gauge shotgun with an extended chamber and extra rounds, and occasionally traveled with an M16 rifle with extra loaded magazines. She had a few run-ins with Earl and told me that if he got within fifteen feet of her again, even today, she would shoot him. She called him a sleazebag, then said she did not want to be quoted by name. She feared retribution.

When I reminded her that Earl had died several years ago, she told me simply, "He's been dead before."

Twice Earl got caught pothunting. The first time, in 1986, he revealed that he would do just about anything to avoid the consequences of his actions. To escape conviction he ratted on a handful of people around Blanding with pothunted material, some of them distinguished residents, some his own family members. They all had one thing in common: Earl had a grudge against them. He went free while federal agents raided the people on his list, sort of a deal with the devil. More than three hundred pre-Columbian vessels were confiscated, and people in Blanding still tell stories about doors crashing in and the flash of guns. An agent who was part of the sting shrugs at that. He remembers it differently, saying, "We were hardly jackbooted Nazis. We were all in sports jacket and ties; no doors were knocked down. If it was locked, we got a locksmith."

The second time he was caught, however, Earl was not able to deflect the charges. This time he was saddled with a five-year prison sentence—then the biggest antiquities penalty ever handed down in the States (a cigarette butt bearing his DNA was found at one of the digs, and it proved to be his undoing).

The last I heard of his working career, Earl had gotten out of prison and was digging up north, in Labyrinth Canyon in the Green River area. He was supposedly running a mining claim, but with the many prehistoric weaving cultures that used to live in the area, it is easy to guess what he was doing. A couple of years later I heard he had died of cancer. Nobody I knew seemed to know exactly when. Though I've not seen the actual death certificate, a relative of his working at the San Juan County health department vouched that Earl is indeed dead.

. . .

Culture moves slowly in the old and mostly Mormon farming and mining communities scattered around the Four Corners. Something as significant as the 1986 raids takes decades to settle out. Winston Hurst is a local archaeologist who has had to deal with the aftermath. Raised Mormon in Blanding, Hurst traces his mother's local lineage back to 1880 and his father's to 1910. When he talked to me, he looked tired.

"I'm never sure whether to laugh, cry, or puke when I think about this stuff," Hurst said.

A sun-weathered middle-aged man, Hurst was at the

Edge of the Cedars Museum in Blanding, where he spends many of his days engaged in research. In one of the storage rooms where confiscated artifacts are kept, he led me down aisles of shelves explaining that the pots, sandals, and fired effigies around us once belonged to his neighbors.

Like so many here, Hurst also grew up pothunting, but his parents expressed a quiet dislike for unruly excavation. They were sad to see old and familiar sites destroyed. Still, as a kid he pothunted a couple of graves and kept entire human skeletons in the pantry next to the canned peaches. (His mother, not surprisingly, found this vulgar.) He said, "At the heart of it there's always been this explore-and-discover treasure-hunt sort of thing. I think it's fundamental to human instinct."

Over time, Hurst's inquiries became more scientific. He and his brother even employed a microscope to study artifacts they had collected, though he now admits he had not the slightest clue what to do with the microscope. It at least looked scientific. Hurst went on to study archaeology at Brigham Young University, taking classes along with a childhood friend from Blanding, a pothunter with a similar interest in the past. In the end, his friend returned to quiet pothunting while Hurst took the path of professional archaeologist, publishing papers and cataloguing sites. He has since become a leading field scholar, one with a unique, ethnographic knowledge of his landscape.

Hurst said, "When things are done right and an artifact is collected with its context documented in some detail, that documentation travels with the artifact. The information is curated, and the museum maintains it in perpetuity. The connection between the object and the ground is saved. That's a whole different thing than when you take it and stick it on some shelf or you sell it to a stockbroker in New York. That just pops that connection between object and ground. It sterilizes the ground and strips the artifact of its information."

Hurst sees artifacts as pixels on a screen. If you have enough pixels you can make out the picture, but if many are missing the image fades.

He pointed out a black-on-red jar above eye level on a shelf. Tall and somewhat slender, painted red like blush, its ceramic handle was shaped into an animal, perhaps a coyote, and for eyes it bore two striking turquoise beads. He said it had been confiscated from the man who had attended Brigham Young with him. It was a pothunted piece, one of the lost pixels. The jar had been a prize, a lifetime achievement for a digger who passionately scoured the canyons looking for hidden and enchanting objects. Hurst looked at it with a resigned expression. He said people still felt deep animosity about the 1986 raids.

There are those in town who say the museum is in cahoots with the government, taking away people's collections in order to fill its shelves, and that archaeologists are simply another layer of agents who break down doors. Those who had the money fought in court and got some of their prized possessions back. Those who did not have the money lost everything.

"It's painful to me every time I see an artifact leave the ground and go anywhere," Hurst admitted. "Whether it's into somebody's private collection or even into a museum. At this point, I'd rather see it in the ground."

Hurst's desire goes beyond science. He considers how one should treat the history of a place. You don't just take whatever you want. He believes these artifacts belong not to private individuals or even to a discipline, but to a landscape and its past. I once walked with him through a local canyon where we paused to look at the deep oval shadow of a cave overhead. It was called Baby Mummy Cave and had been dug illegally. A mummified infant was left exposed. Dead babies, it turns out, make for rewarding digs. You can pretty much guarantee that a baby will be wrapped in a woven blanket, which on its own can fetch $4,000 (assuming you are in with the local network of black-market buyers, who can either launder it over to a gallery, put it up on eBay, or hang it behind glass on their own wall). The blanket is just the start; dig a little more and you will often come upon an assembly of lovingly crafted necklaces and vessels that can elevate one burial to $10,000 for a savvy pothunter.

Hurst told me that he had gone up to the cave shortly after the looting. He said coyotes had gotten to it, and parts of the baby mummy had been torn off. He swept the pieces together and tucked them back into the dust so they would at least be buried. It was all he could do. I did not ask him why, as a scientist, he resisted moving the remains to a more secure location for study. We both knew why.

. . .

After the 1986 raids, pothunting continued in the Four Corners, but more quietly. Diggers backfilled their holes, smoothing over evidence so it would look as if no one had been there. The swashbuckling capers of Earl Shumway eventually faded; no one wanted to attract suspicion. But the digging was still not quiet enough. Federal investigators kept a close, undercover eye on what was happening in Blanding and the surrounding area. They sent in an informant who moved freely through the local network, wearing a wire while purchasing 256 artifacts over a two-year period for a total of $335,685. The informant (under contract with the FBI and paid $224,000) was a friend of many of the pothunters, so trusted that they openly admitted where the digging had happened, getting out maps and producing photographs, something they would never have done for a stranger. That information made for damning indictments that far exceeded Earl Shumway's testimony from 1986. This time, twenty-six people in Blanding and surrounding communities were targeted, their privacy shattered by 132 secretly recorded conversations that are disturbing in their frankness. Old men impassioned by archaeology told their heartfelt secrets. Discussing where to park a truck so it wouldn't be seen, one pothunter was taped saying he thought they were being paranoid. Another replied that when you're doing something illegal, it's probably good to be paranoid.

At one point, the informant bought a basket for $4,750 from a Blanding man. The seller was a fifty-five-year-old Shumway who explained that he got it out of a burial from Dark Canyon. During the transaction, the seller smelled the inside of the basket, which had been a grave offering. "Can you smell that?" he asked. "It's still there. It makes me want to get back out there, but this is getting spooky, it's all spooky."

The deal came down in June of 2009. This time, agents showed up with shackles and handcuffs, their guns drawn. Just like twenty-three years earlier, the bull's-eye was Blanding, where hundreds of agents raided people's homes. Now they were armed with better evidence. Some of those named in the 2009 indictments had been hit back in 1986, but this time they were shut down for good. Many of the indicted were from prominent local families: Redds, Shumways, Lymans. One was a seventy-eight-year-old member of the Utah Tourism Hall of Fame, a friendly face greeting you at the Blanding Visitor Center. Half were in their sixties and seventies, including husband-and-wife teams. Most were manhandled, dragged out of their houses with such force that locals were appalled. They said the show of force was uncalled for, with 150 agents hitting the Blanding area simultaneously.

The operation was officially called Cerberus Action. Cerberus was a monstrous three-headed dog from Greek and Roman mythology that guards the gates of Hades to keep the dead from escaping. That is how the federal image was presented, as a cutthroat beast charged with keeping the dead in the ground. It was a stark warning to anyone still clinging to the belief that artifacts are anyone's for the taking.

The Blanding town physician, a cherished elder known as Dr. Redd, was one of those indicted. It was no secret around town that the sixty-year-old Redd and his wife, who was also targeted in the raid, were pothunters. They lived in a large house built on a prominent hill overlooking town; few ever got inside to peruse its contents. The couple had faced gravedigging charges in the 1990s, when they were caught shoveling at a prehistoric site south of Blanding. After a six-year legal battle, charges against Dr. Redd were dropped and his wife pleaded no contest for a reduced charge. In 2003 they paid $10,000 to the state, settling related charges. In the 2009 raid, Dr. Redd was released the next day with enough evidence against him that it was clear the charges would stick. His daughter was about to be dragged into it, too. The next morning, Dr. Redd was found dead, parked on his property in his Jeep. He had gassed himself. Community members gathered at the foot of the Redds' driveway, some weeping, some deeply angered, saying agents had gone too far in a town where pothunting was once a respectable part of life. Just about everyone in the area knew Dr. Redd had been a pothunter and kept a fine collection of artifacts, so why did he kill himself when it went public? It might help to understand that in Mormon culture, public denouncement can be socially devastating. Dr. Redd's case was not so much a matter of guilt but shame. His private affairs were now known to the world, perhaps enough to drive a leading figure to suicide.

Dr. Redd's death was followed a little over a week later by that of another defendant, a fifty-six-year-old from nearby Durango, Colorado, named Steven Shrader, who had already turned himself in. Not one of the big diggers, he was more peripheral, a sidekick. Instead of showing up for his arraignment in Salt Lake City, Shrader drove to Illinois, where his mother lived, and at 10:45 that night—his mother knew the time because she heard gunshots in the distance—he shot himself twice in the chest behind an elementary school.

A war of editorials broke out as more people were indicted. In Blanding, one angry redneck was arrested for openly stating that he wanted to tie the informant to a tree and beat him with a baseball bat. A new T-shirt showed up in town reading "Kiss My Artifact." Suddenly you could hardly find a privately held pre-Columbian artifact on display in the Four Corners region as items were pulled from motel lobbies and gas station windows. Every scrap of potential evidence was hidden. Durango's historic Strater Hotel scuttled the tasteful display case of whole vessels that it had kept in a well-lit entry hall. In a strange way, it was like watching archaeology disappear all over again.

Cerberus Action went beyond Blanding and the Four Corners to ensnare anyone the informant had been able to contact. An attorney living near Denver who collected stone artifacts as a hobby had been called ten times by the informant, who entreated him to come dig. Though the attorney ultimately declined, he admitted over the phone to picking up potsherds in Utah, which tangled him up in the raid.

Vern and Marie Crites, who lived in Durango, had one of the largest collections, and the raid hit them with seven felony charges. Two felonies stemmed from an identical pair of burial sandals, one charge per sandal. Five moving vans showed up at their house while a busy crowd of agents and archaeologists removed thousands upon thousands of artifacts, stacking boxes on the lawn and flash-cataloguing everything they could pick up (their likely destination select museums and repatriations to tribes). While the Criteses voluntarily surrendered the collection, they pleaded that nearly all of it came from private land, from either their own local ranch or someone else's property, which under U.S. law is legal (as long as it does not involve burial, a difficult distinction to prove beyond a doubt). The Criteses watched decades of their personal passion go out the door. According to the warrant, Vern was a dealer who had boasted of selling sets of pottery for up to $500,000 each, and according to other players caught in the sting, he was a key "price setter." The collection removed from his house consisted of pieces gathered over fifty years, some of the finest ceramic specimens found in the Southwest: bulging globes of painted jars, mugs decorated with animal effigies, ornately decorated bowls. Many of these pieces he was not willing to sell. At one point during the confiscation, the lead investigator turned to seventy-four-year-old Vern and told him that in jail he wasn't going to need any of this.

Vern had not only been caught on tape admitting to illegal acts, he had been observed by a surveillance team of Bureau of Land Management agents as he dug a grave on federal land alongside the informant and another pothunter. Together they found a human skull on the third shovelful. They picked up the skull, then put it back in the ground and covered it over with dirt, deciding to end their dig there.

Judy Seiler, the Criteses' adult niece, who grew up in this digging culture, called me repeatedly to defend her uncle and aunt. "The feds didn't catch the big sellers or buyers," she said. "These are salt of the earth people who just can't bear the humiliation of what's happened. My uncle knew more about archaeology than just about anyone. He had a relationship with it. It was his life."

Judy's voice over the phone was steady and intelligent, but brimming with anger. She had witnessed her uncle's museumlike house being emptied, a major piece of her own childhood suddenly lost, a beloved elderly uncle exposed. "You're watching the destruction of a human being," Judy said. "Do you realize what this does to these people? My friend Steven Shrader shot himself over it. This is what it means to them. This is humiliation you cannot understand. These are simple, good people."

What are good people doing digging graves? "He should have stayed off federal land," Judy said. "But the rest of that stuff is lawfully his. He was truly taking care of it. You have to understand, this is love. Farmers in the tens and twenties would use pots for target practice, potshots. There were millions of artifacts, for Christ's sake, millions of them. The next generation, my uncle comes along and reveres these things. He puts them under lock and key. You sell them on the side, you move some along. It's not the dollar amount— it's where it goes, who appreciates it, who keeps it. Where do you draw the line? We are living on top of cultures. You have a ranch and you are not supposed to plow? Instead of plowing, he gathered. He couldn't destroy these things. This is our passion. Why should we be assaulted for it? You tell me where the hypocrisy lies."

The last time Judy called—before she said the case attorneys finally advised her to stop—she was coolly livid as she named people all the way up the ranks, talking about a conspiracy she believed went from the Southern Ute tribe to the head of the Department of the Interior. She was pushing legal action, taking donations, saying she would not give up until she exonerated her uncle as well as her friend who had fired two bullets into his own chest.

Some say that the damage to the artifact culture is irreparable, a unique knowledge of a landscape and its buried history crushed. Others say getting off with fines, losing their collections, and plea-bargaining their way out of jail time represents a mere slap on the wrist for people who have swiped pieces of the archaeological record. When Dr. Redd's wife and thirty-seven-year-old daughter escaped jail time with probation, receiving fines of $2,000 and $300 respectively, an Archaeological Conservancy spokesman said, "I'm afraid it sends a message that this is not serious criminal activity." But jackbooted federal raids and national press coverage certainly made it look serious.

In the spring of 2010, just as some of the first trials were set to begin, police were called to the informant's house outside Salt Lake City, where the fifty-two-year-old man who had acted as the sole undercover operative was threatening suicide. He had a gun and appeared dangerously belligerent. Police called in a SWAT team. By the time they found him, the informant had gone into his bedroom and, with one bullet, taken his own life.

This third suicide raised serious legal doubt as to whether the cases could even be prosecuted, the star witness dead. When Bureau of Land Management agents arrived in Blanding to continue the investigation, the sheriff told them just to leave and never come back. The raids were meant to push pothunting farther from the realm of acceptability. What they created was a besieged, rancorously divided community and a string of deaths, making many locals even less willing to cooperate. Divisions have grown only deeper, the artifact underworld slipping farther out of range.

Judy was right about the raids. Only the easiest targets were caught, mostly old-school diggers. Who they did not catch were aerial investors and those actively traveling from site to site with industrious efficiency, people far too savvy to let their names slip to locals. I've come close to some of these high-skill diggers, but only close enough for them to relay that they are not willing to talk. They do not have time for Indiana Jones antics or waxing rhapsodic about their endeavors. They're too busy moving and hiding, supplying a distant market that seems to have no bottom.

CHAPTER 6

GOING TO MARKET

Diggers who sell have one thing in common. They dig because there is demand. Antiquities are one of the top illegal trades in the world. The international sale of illicit artifacts is estimated somewhere between $4 billion and $8 billion a year. Once you get beyond the local mom-and-pop outfits, you have entered a global arena and a much more profitable market.

On the world stage, artifacts from the American Southwest make up a dependable but relatively backwoods commerce. Meanwhile, diggers in Central America are trenching into monumental city-states rather than villages, and tombs instead of graves. The money is much bigger, and so is the scale of looting. In Guatemala, crews are employed to find Mayan artifacts for powerful dealers, gangs, and smuggling rings. Some diggers are leftover guerrillas roaming the jungle in military fatigues, weapons slung on their backs as they work in teams out of any number of base camps hidden in the jungle. They put the boisterous work of the late Earl Shumway to shame as they target certain architectural groupings and types of ruins where they know they will find quick money. In one day they can dig a formidable tunnel, prop it up with chopped-down hardwoods, empty a tomb, and be gone. Archaeologists and museums have hired guards to protect certain sites, but in one instance, two guards in the Petén region of eastern Guatemala were found eviscerated, their corpses hung from trees.

Not all Central American looters are dangerous or belong to well-organized teams. Many are blue-collar locals dressed in T-shirts or sweaty button-downs. They dig trenches and tunnels, earning five to ten dollars a day at best, turning Mayan artifacts into bread, fuel, and new televisions. Contractors sometimes provide mules and supplies to a group of locals heading out for a two-week foray and pay them based on what they bring back. The contractors then move artifacts to middleman buyers who may or may not be the smugglers, taking the remaining profit for themselves (which is minimal compared to what the next set of hands makes). Rarely do the diggers ever see the client who buys the artifacts, and they never meet the end buyer who at auction is willing to pay $200,000 for a painted Mayan vessel or a foot-tall stone carving.

Most of the grunt work happens within a Third World subsistence environment in which locals are accustomed to using the jungle's resources—gum, timber, and temples alike. In villages or work camps throughout the Petén you see humble pre-Columbian bowls reused on eating tables or ancient ceramic jars employed as a water dippers. Intricately carved stones weighing tons have been found broken into slabs for village fire hearths. These are the ones that didn't go to market, that are not good enough for sale.

Sales out of Central America first really picked up in the 1960s, when Mayan artifacts started rising in popularity among museums and private collectors. Within a couple of decades the digging and smuggling industry in Central America had become entrenched. Richard Hansen, a lead archaeologist in the Petén, has been ambitious in his attempts to stop this looting, posting armed guards at his sites and trying to hire every able-bodied villager for field-work, sometimes 340 people at a time. He figures that if they are working for him they won't be digging for the black market.

In the 1990s Hansen witnessed the very peak: the illegal departure from the Petén of a thousand or more prized poly-chrome vessels every month, an export he estimated to be worth $120 million a year. That export, he says, has steadily declined. Is this a sign of success on the part of conserva-tionists like himself? Hansen says no.

"I believe the flow is less now for the simple fact that most of the sites in the Petén have been horribly desecrated and destroyed," Hansen says. "Where I have guards, we still have intact architecture and cities, but, barring that, the devastation is horrendous."

The last fresh Mayan artifacts to land on the black mar-ket are now being sent mostly to the United States, along with a strong flow to Europe, particularly Belgium. They are packaged, concealed, and loaded on container ships or smuggled by hand across borders, seeding the globe with lost bits of Mesoamerica.

William Saturno, another leading archaeologist in the Petén, once told me that when he and his colleagues enter sites being actively plundered, the looters have always been kind enough to back away. Saturno has been using satellite images to find undocumented ruins in the jungle, detecting them by tracking vegetative patterns (limestone architecture and lime plaster alter what grows there, rendering them vis-ible even through the jungle canopy), and when he has gone to ground-truth, or verify, even remote ones (there are thou-sands) he says he invariably finds them already carved open by looters.

When he talks about the people who dig illegal trenches,

Saturno does not use invectives, speaking of them as you might describe neighbors you need to get along with. Saturno said most of the looters he has met would rather be doing other work, if there were enough other paying work to do. But the rainy season occupies a big chunk of the year, and it is a lean period when people take looting jobs even though they know the work is dangerous (tunnels frequently collapse). Many were trained on official archaeological projects going back to the 1970s, and some have even worked as guards. Saturno said the ones he has come to know take no pleasure in destroying Mayan archaeology. "It is about simple economy," he said.

The limestone here is soft enough that it can be cut with a chain saw, which reduces these cities to manageable dimensions. With this added level of portability, looters have taken not only tomb contents, but entire pieces of architecture. Prominent Mayan stelae weighing up to sixty-five tons have been unfaced by the thousands, their glyph-covered surfaces representing easy sales (some have even been converted into coffee tables). Two stelae that received this chain-saw treatment can be seen at the Cleveland Art Museum and the Kimbell Art Museum in Fort Worth, Texas. Originally the two were beside each other in the once-great Mayan city of El Waka-Peru in the northern Petén. One is a depiction of King K'inch B'ahlam II, Sun-Faced Jaguar, and the other is his wife, Lady K'ab'el. It is believed they were taken in the 1960s by a Mexican logger who crossed the border into Guatemala with a chain saw, found these two stelae, cut them down, and hauled them out on mules. They were purchased by the museums around 1970, just before it was made illegal to do so. (In 2009, responding to demands from Guatemala to return these artifacts, the Kimbell actually made a replica of its stela and sent it to Guatemala to replace the original on-site. The Cleveland museum has so far remained silent.)

International crackdowns at the buying end have slowed the illegal exportation of these large stone carvings in the past few decades, and in turn, the demand for more easily transported Mayan pottery and smaller artifacts has increased. Instead of cutting up architecture, looters have focused more on raiding tombs and buried sites.

The end result is that Central America is just about gutted. It is not alone. Asia looks similar, as do Africa, the Middle East, the Mediterranean, parts of North America, and huge tracts of South America. In southern Iraq a recent survey of nearly two thousand sites found that every single one had been dug. Everyplace on earth where human generations have lived is being taken. The Petén in Guatemala was one of the first to go down, with other regions quickly following.

How does it all work once artifacts leave the diggers? The black market that collects and disseminates these goods may seem impenetrable, but to see it, you need only peek behind the curtain.

. . .

If there is rent to pay on a showroom, an antiquities dealer has got to have steady turnover, new artifacts arriving on a regular basis so that the same dusty statue will not be seen for sale year after year. New artifacts have to come from somewhere, and many arrive through apparently legal means, either in circulation before the advent of antiquities laws or pulled from private collections in English manors and Indian trade shops. These are what make the business legal. How do you tell the difference between legal artifacts and those recently dug and laundered? You pretty much can't, which is why professional dealers can work in the open, above the black market. A Santa Fe dealer once told me that half his collection was probably illegal, he just did not know which half.

Here in a nutshell is how the global black market works. Freeport warehouses in Switzerland are signed over to fictitious businesses that pick up shipments from Egypt, Mali, Delhi, and Hong Kong and get out before a trace can be made. In India a common practice is to make replicas of looted objects, have them assessed by archaeological authorities who sign them off as fakes, then supply the real ones with this paperwork so they can slip through customs without a hitch. The artifacts are sometimes bought and sold between shell corporations to further obscure their origins, and with essentially new identities they move into the hands of auction houses and art dealers, their paperwork nearly impeccable. Voilà, they become legal, all traces of the black market obliterated so that antiquities can fly around the world in a nonstop migration.

Sometimes a paper trail is found, or a smuggler testifies. The wrong object can blow up into search warrants, Interpol investigations, confiscation, prison time. Private collectors, museum heads, even archaeologists get caught in these traps. A respected dealer in Southeast Asian art was exposed in 2003 for running a multimillion-dollar illicit antiquities business, one of the largest in the world, that was hidden behind a craft showroom in Jaipur. Repercussions from his arrest extended around the world, exposing private buyers and collectors in the United States, Britain, and Switzerland. All those caught pleaded that these objects were bought in good faith. But good faith is almost meaningless now. Lies disappear into the chain of hands, and you can rarely know whom to trust.

With other objects, however, the value and prestige goes

nowhere but up. These are the ones with clean records, ones that raise little or no international suspicion. Who knows, they may even be legal to start with, objects that entered the trade early, before antiquities laws went on the books. The trick is knowing when to grab hold of these and when to let go.

The late Thomas Hoving, a sharp-eyed and audacious art connoisseur from the United States, moved in and out of this game adroitly. Born into the jewelry-store barony of Tiffany & Co., Hoving developed keen aesthetic sensibilities and a penchant for antiquities. He worked as an archaeologist excavating sites in Italy in the 1950s, building his knowledge of Greek antiquities from the ground up, and there he inadvertently trained a man who would later become a master smuggler. (Hoving could not rightly say if he had ever bought from the man, explaining that smugglers excel at covering up their tracks.)

Hoving eventually became a curator for the Metropolitan Museum of Art in New York, and later took the position of director from 1967 to 1977, by far the museum's most glamorous and outrageous years. He flabbergasted trustees with the prices he paid for artifacts, embarrassed them with arrogant blunders, and soundly alienated other museums. An acquaintance of his once told me Hoving was too wily and slippery to ever be taken down. "He knows what to protect and what can break," this source said, adding that nobody was ever going to cut off Hoving's horns or clip his balls.

At the height of his museum career in the 1970s, while curator and director of the Metropolitan, Hoving jumped ship and went from being a self-described buyer of smuggled antiquities to a voice against the traffic. He helped draft an antismuggling treaty in 1970, the now famous UNESCO Convention on the Means of Prohibiting and Preventing the Illicit Import, Export and Transfer of Ownership of

Cultural Property. The first and most powerful global convention of its kind, this treaty was intended to halt the flow of unprovenanced artifacts across international borders and had to be ratified country by country. With it, the division between right and wrong was made plain: if the origin of an artifact is not clearly documented and it was bought after 1970, it is considered loot. By purchasing this loot, the treaty declared, you are also buying the destruction of history.

Hoving described himself to me as having once been a pirate. He said he used to laugh at provenance, proud of the fact that he had been able to move dubious antiquities out of Italy and into the Cloisters at the Metropolitan. What changed?

"I realized that the time had come to stop the old age of piracy," he said, "and that we ought to get together and slow down—you never can stop it—the unauthorized, unprovenanced market of antiquities.

"You have to be perceptive about watershed changes," Hoving told me. It was not that he wanted to avoid ruffling feathers. He simply saw where the market was heading and was wise enough to move into the lead. Countries were beginning to demand that their cultural heritages remain within their borders, not flung to the world. By 1970 some countries, namely Italy, had started gaining real political clout, and Hoving could see that the tide was turning.

Hoving was also widely known as the man who purchased the smuggled Euphronios krater for what was then an astonishing $1 million. He bought it in 1972, two years after the promulgation of the UNESCO treaty, but six years before Italy (the source of the krater) actually ratified it. When Hoving saw the door closing with the UNESCO treaty being ratified by key countries, he grabbed the best artifact he could find and jumped through.

The Euphronios krater is essentially a mixing bowl used

to hold several gallons of wine and water. Made around 515 BC, it is the size of a cauldron, and it is considered by many the finest vessel to come out of Greek antiquity. It came to Hoving's attention in 1971 through an acclaimed dealer, the elder statesman of smugglers Robert Hecht, whom Hoving had dealt with for years. From the moment the transaction began, Hoving believed the krater had been looted and taken illegally from Italy (he was most likely correct). It had been broken and flawlessly repaired, missing not even a sliver, which meant that it had likely been intentionally damaged so it could be packed small in order to cross international borders without drawing attention.

In his own zestfully written account, published in 2001 in the online magazine *artnet* and in his book *Making the Mummies Dance,* Hoving wrote of a controversial exchange he had back in 1971 with the Metropolitan's curator of Greek and Roman art, Dr. Dietrich von Bothmer, as the two men flew to Zurich to see the krater for the first time. Hoving had asked von Bothmer where he thought the krater came from. Von Bothmer's response was to say nothing.

Hoving wrote, "I at once interpreted Dietrich's silence as his knowing the thing was illegal. At that moment he and I established an unspoken understanding. We would avoid knowledge of the history of the vase. We would never talk about where we really thought was its provenance."

To sell it cleanly, Hecht told Hoving the krater came from an antiquities dealer in Beirut who had had it in his family since at least 1914 — which later turned out to be false, but which would have dated it to well before laws imposed by Italy or UNESCO, implying it was legal. Lebanon, not party to the treaty, was a convenient source for the krater. According to what Hecht cooked up, the artifact appeared legitimate, its fictitious provenance strong enough to pass muster with attorneys.

In Zurich, acting as buyers for the Metropolitan, Hoving and von Bothmer found the krater in the house of a supposed furniture restorer, a place loaded with antiquities in various states of repair. When Hoving first caught sight of the piece, he was overwhelmed by its scale and elegance, and struck by the fine paintings girdling it: winged, helmeted gods lifting the bleeding body of Sarpedon, the son of Zeus killed in battle. A luminous black glaze surrounded the reddish figures. On the other side he saw an electrifying scene of beautifully muscled warriors dressing for battle. Hoving had to have the krater. He said it was the single most perfect and powerful work of art of its size he had ever encountered. Only the most neurotically ethical buyer would have been able to step away from this one.

Once word got out that the Met had dropped $1 million for a single artifact, the market took off, and a heightened wave of looting and smuggling started. Intended or not, Hoving's purchase—essentially on the morning after the antismuggling UNESCO treaty—triggered a black-market cascade, a sudden rush of investors toward antiquities. The treaty's restrictions coupled with the explosive need for new artifacts created a bottleneck, the foundation for the current artifact market.

Italy strongly objected to Hoving's purchase, and the *New York Times* did its damnedest to uncover wrongdoing, yet in the 1970s the deal looked surprisingly untouchable. Zurich was the ideal conduit for moving the Euphronios krater into the United States. In 1972 Switzerland, a country known for its leniency toward underground traffic, was not even considering signing the UNESCO treaty (even the United States did not officially recognize it until 1983).

Almost two decades after Hoving abandoned his post at the Metropolitan, UNESCO caught up with the rest of the world, and even Switzerland got in on the action, signing the convention in 2003. Italian and Swiss investigators raided a Geneva warehouse in 1995 and brought down an antiquities smuggling ring that led them to Hecht. In Hecht's Paris apartment they came up with enough material to lead them to the conclusion that the Euphronios krater had nothing to do with the supposed Beirut dealer. The krater, they charged, was acquired in 1971 by a crew of looters at an Etruscan tomb near San Antonio di Cerveteri in Italy. In 2008, after years of legal battles and negotiations, the Metropolitan finally gave up the Euphronios and sent it back to Italy.

I asked Hoving if he saw any contradiction about having bought the Euphronios after being part of the UNESCO treaty, and he snapped at me, saying I obviously didn't know anything about it.

"It was years before we found out the krater was smuggled," he said brusquely.

But hadn't Hoving written that he knew it was smuggled when he bought it? No, not exactly. He said he had merely *believed* it was smuggled, a notion he and von Bothmer decided to keep to themselves for the longest time. The difference between *believing* and actually *knowing* it was smuggled was enough to put him in the ethical clear, at least in Hoving's mind. I asked him if any blame was attached to him and he told me that Hecht had "bamboozled" him.

When I spoke with Hoving, he was seventy-seven years old and the krater had just gone back to Rome, supposedly for good. Almost four decades had passed since his suspicious purchase, and in that time the antiquities world had changed markedly, one could say thanks to Hoving's own hand.

When Hoving started working to stop the illegal trade (when it suited him, apparently), he became a loose cannon among institutions, a former insider taking strong positions against museums that were buying artifacts with questionable provenances. He fingered the J. Paul Getty Museum in Los Angeles, declaring that a sculpture of Aphrodite bought by the Getty in 1988 for $18 million had been looted from Morgantina, Sicily, and eventually it was repatriated. He took personal credit for getting the museum's curator Jiri Frel fired in 1984 for blundering excesses. (At a dinner with Frel in Rome, Hoving claims the enraged former curator snatched a bottle of mineral water and began striking him with it until waiters and patrons jumped in and stopped the fray.)

From there the dominoes continued to fall. The Getty was caught holding artifacts that, like the Euphronios krater, had come through Robert Hecht. Italy, inflamed with its new power in the global artifacts arena, demanded justice, and both Hecht and the Getty's new head curator, Marion True, were indicted and stood trial in Rome, and their trial is ongoing.

Hoving laughed about Marion True and the Getty debacle. "They had it coming," he said.

He laughed, too, when I asked him how he felt about Italy finally forcing the Metropolitan to give back the Euphronios krater.

"Museums have too much shit anyway," he said.

Hoving envisioned a brave new world of artifacts being exchanged rather than sitting under the thumb of curators in large metropolitan museums. When the Getty decided to send artifacts back, it signed an agreement of exchange with the Italian culture ministry that allowed the museum to receive long-term loans of artifacts. The Metropolitan made a similar move, accepting a rotation of artifacts in return for the Euphronios and other pieces.

Put simply, Hoving was a shit stirrer. Listening to his

catty eloquence and his degrading quips, you realized he must have been like a bomb going off in the staid world of antiquities.

. . .

Complain as one might about the buying and selling of the past, the fact remains that there is a legitimate antiquities market. It is part of international art commerce, a free flow of publicly owned artifacts—such as those from St. Lawrence Island and other pockets of legal sources—that has been going on for as long as there have been early cultures to root around in. These artifacts, at least most of those acquired before 1970, can move openly across many borders, bought and sold in broad daylight. For the countless miscellany of vases, bells, and statues, it is almost impossible to tell the difference between those that are fundamentally legal and those laundered beyond recognition.

Artifact prices on the open market are soaring. Speculation is the primary element determining value, which allows prices to go outrageously high on a whim. In 2007, a 5,000-year-old Mesopotamian limestone figurine the size of a chess piece, of a lion in a human pose, was publicly auctioned. It started with an opening bid of $8.5 million and four bidders quickly elevated it to $27 million (it was not expected to go over $18 million). Finally an anonymous gray-suited English gentleman standing in the back of the room lifted his paddle and carried the bid up to $57.2 million and took the artifact home.

Everything in the figurine's record-breaking sale was legal, the relevant records open to the public. The artifact had been on loan to the Brooklyn Museum of Art since 1948, until the actual owner, the museum's former president of the board, decided to pull it from display and put it up for auction at Sotheby's. The auction house called it one of the "last known masterworks from the dawn of civilization remaining in private hands."

Noting a sudden escalation in the market brought on by this figurine, *Time* magazine ran an article putting antiquities at the top of its list for discretionary investments. The article made sure to say that you need not be scared away by million-dollar price tags. For under $10,000 you too can be a successful player in the antiquities market by legally buying two to four quality artifacts from a dealer, flipping them at a profit, then buying and selling more expensive pieces, and so on. The *Time* reporter concluded by saying, "No matter how ornate a stock certificate might be, an Egyptian amulet is always going to look better in your living room display case."

This statement stunned archaeologists, who carped at the magazine, saying it failed to mention downsides such as countries losing their cultural heritage, looters ransacking history, and an underworld where artifacts are being moved by some of the same people who handle guns and drugs.

Indeed, legal sales are a veneer spurring greater demand, which inevitably results in more digging and smuggling to push fresh artifacts onto the market. How do you keep a market legitimate when it causes the last tombs to be raided? It is a precarious ethical balance dealers live with.

Hicham Aboutaam, part owner of the prestigious New York City and Geneva gallery Phoenix Ancient Art, once told me he does everything in his legal power to track provenance before he buys or sells. He said that it behooves him to acquire only legal artifacts. This master antiquities dealer adds, however, "It would be naive to say we can know everything, especially when it comes to the many smaller works of art. Who out there is willing to spend more money on lawyers than the actual value of the piece?"

Aboutaam, now one of the most powerful public dealers

in the world, grew up in Beirut, where his father was successful in the same line of work. He was raised in a house full of artifacts he considered both the basis of his education and his toys. He began collecting at the age of thirteen, first seals and scarabs, then Roman and Greek antiquities.

The antiquities business used to be very different, though: artifacts sold in back rooms, museum curators drifting in and out, buying as if they could not get enough. The antismuggling laws on the books were lightweight, and dealers who violated them could put up a jewelry store or a furnishing business as a front, and get away without much hassle.

Times have changed. Now that UNESCO's convention and heaps of newer laws have taken effect, antiquities dealers are probed to the point where they have to either go deeper underground or go public. Entering the public spotlight with full-color aplomb, as Aboutaam has done with his highly visible sales, can be risky. Aboutaam has not had an especially easy go of it. In 2001 it was reported that the Kimbell Art Museum in Fort Worth returned a Sumerian statue it had bought from Phoenix Ancient Art for $2.7 million, citing purported tax problems with the object. The gallery refunded the purchase price. Then, in 2003, Phoenix forfeited a $20,000 alabaster stela when the piece went up for auction at Sotheby's. The auction house, which has since hired a former federal art-crimes prosecutor to handle provenance issues, recognized the stela as already belonging to a museum in Yemen, and customs agents quickly seized it. In December of that same year Aboutaam was arrested for providing false documentation while moving a 2,000-year-old silver vessel into the United States, claiming its origin as Syria when it actually came from Iran (he says it was a paperwork error). The Iranian piece had been sold to a private buyer (a trustee for the Metropolitan) for nearly

$950,000, but was seized by the U.S. Department of Homeland Security.

Phoenix Ancient Art then sold a four-foot-high slab of Egyptian limestone covered in hieroglyphs that was later confiscated from a Fifth Avenue apartment amid a tangle of provenance issues, and the gallery had to swallow the $210,000 sale. Aboutaam's brother Ali, who runs the Geneva showroom, was accused of smuggling artifacts from Egypt to Switzerland and was sentenced in absentia to fifteen years in prison by an Egyptian court. He has appealed the charges.

The rap sheet for Phoenix Ancient Art is impressive, but not wildly so for a high-profile gallery moving artifacts reportedly worth in excess of $40 million a year. It is the cost of doing business. "We are seeing auction houses conducting more due diligence than in the past," Aboutaam told me. "Among dealers and museums there are many more questions about the ownership history of the pieces transacted, and objects are being rejected by a number of buyers. All of these things did not exist—or if they did it was subtle—fifteen or twenty years ago."

Aboutaam speaks with a rich accent, his words casual but deliberately chosen. He is a clean-cut Lebanese entrepreneur, and though he politely declines the title, he has become the new face of the antiquities business as he strives to make his work more visible, publishing glossy journals featuring the artifacts he is selling and retaining a powerful public relations firm to care for his company's image. With measured humility he said, "I am working on getting the antiquities trade more public, exposed."

No longer can brazen and snide men like Hoving rule the market. Now one must be savvy on another level, presenting a smooth and trustworthy persona while deftly pulling strings. Using transparency as his shield, Aboutaam has opened his gallery to greater scrutiny, but in the end, he says, it is easier than hiding in the shadows.

In May of 2009, Aboutaam's gallery gave back to Italy 251 objects worth $2.7 million. In a bold PR move that suggests how the high-end artifact business might work in the future, the gallery put out a press release stating, "We returned these ancient artifacts in the spirit of cooperation and collaboration with the international art world, and to demonstrate Phoenix's commitment to the preservation and repatriation of national treasures to their host countries." The release added, "We have amicably settled the matter with the Italian authorities, and urge others in the art world to follow suit and also the lead of some of the world's great museums such as the Metropolitan Museum of Art and the Museum of Fine Arts in Boston in repatriating antiquities whose provenance may be in doubt." The approach is a curious one, considering that the gallery sold many of those very artifacts to museums in the first place.

To stay out of trouble, Aboutaam explains, you have to ask many questions and take your time with purchases. Good advice, of course, but it is often hard to follow, given how fast artifacts move through the market. He retains two full-time employees just to research provenance.

"Does this make me immune from being lied to?" he asked. "I don't think so."

In 2005, Aboutaam was offered a headless stone statue of a Sumerian king, a small black figure with detailed inscriptions running along its shoulder and back. It happened to be one of the most valuable artifacts stolen from the National Museum of Iraq during the U.S.-led invasion in 2003, after which it was smuggled through Syria and into the States. Aboutaam told the seller he was not interested and contacted federal officials, since this particular statue was on the FBI's list of the top ten most wanted stolen works of art in the world. Although Aboutaam has been quiet about the details, he was instrumental in tracking down the statue, which was eventually recovered and returned to Iraq.

He would rather talk about acquisitions. His voice began purring as he explained that the gallery had purchased a Cycladic idol, a fantastic Aegean grave offering from circa 2500 BC. "An extraordinary object," he said. "It is a male figure. There are said to be only six male figures of this kind in the world. It sort of went unnoticed by most museums and private collectors, and I grabbed it at a seven-digit number."

Aboutaam finds an overarching value in the market because, he says, it keeps history in motion. It pulls the past into the present. Rather than having major artifacts moving invisibly through the black market, Aboutaam wants them to be seen by the public, their history appearing on a larger stage. Certain artifacts he has watched for decades, tracking them through the market or patiently wooing an owner to sell. This idol was one he had long wanted, even though it would be in his possession only briefly before being turned around to another buyer. He wants to be part of its history, to put his hand onto the movement of civilization.

Cycladic idols come from the Early Bronze Age and became popular after World War II. It is estimated that around twelve thousand graves in the Cycladic Islands of the southern Aegean have been opened to find these idols. The slender carvings are notoriously hard to date, as is the exact manner of their use, because they almost all come from private sources rather than from archaeologists. They have almost no documented context. It is ultimately safer for buyers and sellers to obscure or destroy information about where they came from than to preserve archaeological data that could prove incriminating. But like that of most collectors and dealers, Aboutaam's interest transcends strict archaeological definitions. Artistry and antiquity in themselves tell enough of a story to fascinate him. The primal, curved forms of Cycladic idols represent something that traditional science almost misses, a singular, archetypal shape that suggests who we once were as humans. Reams of data and analysis are not required: it is one straight shot to the heart.

"One of these days this idol is going to go back to the public in an institution, and it will be in every book on the history of art," said Aboutaam. "It is what I live for. What our father lived for. I feel privileged and honored helping to make that wonderful work of art available to the public and to scholars and to future generations."

. . .

Only top sellers can afford to be as visible as Aboutaam. Underneath are layers of midrange dealers who work closer to the source of their artifacts. For fifteen years Jon and Cari Markell ran an opulent little Los Angeles showroom called the Silk Roads Gallery. Gregarious with their customers and favored by local museums, they carried a nice selection of Ming and Qing dynasty statuary from China, as well as a full complement of artifacts from the rest of Asia and even some pieces from the American Southwest. One-stop shopping, it was a favorite of Hollywood nabobs, with prices ranging from the low thousands up to $60,000.

In January of 2008, federal agents raided the gallery, brandishing a warrant compiled by an undercover agent the owners had come to trust as a buyer. The warrant stated that for at least ten years Silk Roads had been smuggling looted objects out of Asia, beads, bracelets, and statuary coming to the gallery directly through China, Thailand, and Myanmar by the thousands. Silk Roads was named as the distribution end of an illegal export/import chain. Individual artifacts had been disguised as replicas and bore "Made in Thailand" stickers that were then peeled off in an L.A. storehouse before going on sale. The gallery allegedly sold artifacts to clients at prices sometimes elevated to 400 percent of wholesale and soon afterward arranged for the same artifacts to be donated to museums. The inflated donations would have acted as tax shelters, a perk for customers of Silk Roads. All this was told to the undercover agent by the Markells themselves, and by their key acquisition man, Robert Olson.

At the same moment the gallery was raided, four prominent museums in Southern California were waking up to discover armed federal agents on their lawns. The museums, including the renowned Los Angeles County Museum of Art, had dealt with Silk Roads and their clients. The institutions all claimed ignorance as agents pored over their collections and quizzed them about the provenance of their pieces. They said they had taken these donations in good faith and that the items would have drifted back into the opacity of private collections had they not accepted them. But while museums were claiming good faith, a report from the undercover agent charged that at least one curator had accepted donations while admittedly overlooking paperwork discrepancies that called provenance into question.

Far more than ten thousand objects were confiscated in the raids, many originating in Thailand. Joyce White, a prominent archaeologist in the field of early Thai civilization, was called in to identify them. White is a senior researcher at the University of Pennsylvania Museum, which has had its thumb in Thailand since it began excavating there in 1968 and was the first institution to define some of the most important prehistoric settlements in the world. Early civilization in Thailand dates back to 2000 BC. Known as the Ban Chiang tradition, its artifacts made up much of the Silk Roads haul. White was astonished when she first saw these masses of confiscated artifacts: thousands of bracelets, bells, vessels, and ornate clay rollers. She told me that an entire slice of history, from the late Neolithic through the Iron Age, had been removed from Thailand and deposited in Los Angeles.

If we can assume that most artifacts from the tradition were found post-1961—with Ban Chiang being a fairly recent discovery—then anyone outside Thailand probably has them illegally. Thailand could become the next Italy as it orders the return of its antiquities. The first major repatriation is coming from Robert Olson and the Silk Roads material.

White says her willingness and ability to step into the legal fray is unusual for an archaeologist. In her opinion most of her colleagues avoid knowledge of the antiquities market simply because it is depressing. They are also afraid to put their necks on the line by stating in a trial what an artifact is and where it came from, a decision that could have catastrophic effects on other people's lives.

"The sale of prehistoric objects needs to end," White said firmly. "It's time archaeologists step up to the plate."

White's analysis helped secure the first arrest in the widening probe around the Silk Roads Gallery. Five months after the raid, Roxanna Brown, a sixty-two-year-old curator for the Southeast Asian Ceramics Museum at Bangkok University in Thailand—and one of the leading experts on the ancient pottery of Southeast Asia—was arrested in Seattle. Brown, who moved in some of the same circles as White, had left her home in Bangkok in the winter of 2008 and traveled to the United States for a speaking engagement at the University of Washington. The agents who apprehended her in a hotel room claimed that her electronic signature had been found on appraisals of smuggled Ban Chiang artifacts that vastly inflated their values. She was told that if she was found guilty she faced twenty years in prison for wire fraud, and because of her ties to Bangkok she was deemed a flight risk and held without bail. The experience shattered her. While in custody she became so enfeebled (she had a prosthetic leg, the result of a car accident) that other inmates had to carry her to the shower. On May 14, 2008, not long after her incarceration, an ulcer in her stomach ruptured, and Brown died in her jail cell, choking on her own fluids.

At the time of her arrest, Brown was considered a staunch preservationist, having publicly implored collectors not to purchase unprovenanced artifacts. A friend called her a tireless defender of ethics in the art trade. The kind of research she did—studying ancient ceramics trading in early Southeast Asia—required that she work only with artifacts from 100 percent intact assemblages. Bogus collections were worthless to her: their pieces could have come from anywhere, and she was mapping the trade routes of the time. For this reason Brown worked mainly with shipwrecks, sites she could verify as unpillaged, their dishes still stacked in cupboards drowned at the bottom of the sea.

On a visit to the United States two months before her arrest, Brown had confided in her brother that she was worried about the Silk Roads case. She said she had signed one appraisal for the gallery, but only one, and she had done it by e-mail after scrutinizing photographs of an artifact. But agents found her appraisals on numerous documents. According to her brother, Brown's signature had been hijacked to appear on documentation for artifacts even outside her field of study.

I spoke to Fred Brown a few weeks after his sister's death. He was beside himself, contending she had been caught in a witch hunt. "She went into the field to stop [illegal trade]," he pleaded. "That was the whole point, why she needed a doctoral degree. People were telling her that there was so much corruption that she needed to be high up to stop it."

But the case is not so simple. Brown's contacts and transactions reveal that she was deeply tangled in the antiquities underworld. Brown herself had transported undeclared artifacts from Thailand to the United States and had sold them to the Markells at the Silk Roads Gallery. Polite e-mails between Brown and the Markells attached to the warrant indicate she had a friendly working relationship with the gallery. Brown knew she was in slippery terrain. The Markells wrote to reassure her, telling her not to worry about getting caught: "If you are nervous about doing this, please realize that Republicans are still in office, the IRS does not have enough personnel to review small time appraisals and the appraisals are very well written and will never be challenged even if they do." To which Roxanna responded, "No problem! I am delighted to be your partner in this." At one point the Markells offered $300 for her services as an artifact appraiser. She turned down the cash, later explaining to the agents who apprehended her that she was happy just to help get these artifacts donated to a museum. In confiscated letters, Brown said she had been buying artifacts for the Bangkok museum for which she curated, moving them out of private hands into public collections regardless of provenance, transactions certainly not unheard-of even for major museums in the past (and some would say even now).

Brown also knew Olson, named in the warrant as "the smuggler" supplying Silk Roads with material from Thailand. She told an agent she had been in his storehouse and seen bronze bracelets still hanging from human arm bones, so she had to have known what Olson was up to. In a handwritten letter to him, she reported that she had found a source for Paleolithic artifacts that he should jump on because a London dealer was also interested. She supplied him with lists of available objects and sent out an invoice confirming that she had received $14,000 in cash from him for a prehistoric Thai bell. She added that she was fully prepared to give the money back if the bell was not satisfactory. (Brown eventually assisted a U.S. investigation in which she helped finger Olson—no indictment resulted. She stated that she thought he was the largest and perhaps only commercial U.S. importer of Thai antiquities and that she believed what he was doing was both illegal and wrong.)

Brown was walking a tightrope, part antiquities mule dispersing artifacts from the field and part respected museum conservationist and scholar. On the surface, the two positions may seem incompatible, but if her goal was to assure an optimal state of preservation for antiquities, Brown was probably doing what she believed was best; a lesser evil than letting them vanish into the hodgepodge of middlemen in foreign markets. She was getting objects directly into the hands of a dealer she trusted, knowing that dealer had access to quality museums.

With Brown's death, the Silk Roads case came to a standstill. Olson was not indicted, and neither were the Markells, who took their business out of the gallery and moved it online. Brown remained the only arrest. Her brother told me, "They say she's part of an elaborate scheme. She's not. It's the last thing she said: *I didn't do anything wrong.*" I could not help siding with him in his grief. Roxanna Brown has become an unwitting poster child for the ethical dilemmas of antiquities. But whether she knew it or not, Brown was indeed part of an elaborate scheme, less a scandal than simply part of the landscape. It goes well beyond the Silk Roads Gallery, beyond Aboutaam and Hoving, into a hunger for the past that resides at the seat of the human experience, and it has been around much longer than any of these characters.

CHAPTER 7

A HISTORY OF URGES

It used to be much cleaner. You would grab a chisel and a pith helmet and go to whatever country you liked, and as long as you could afford a caravan and had a working knowledge of weaponry to fend off bandits or angry locals, you were in. There were even places where you did not need a gun. In the nineteenth century, colonial Brits were using the Taj Mahal as a picnic ground, and as one early witness recalled, "revellers [would] arm themselves with hammer and chisel, with which they whiled away the afternoon by chipping out fragments of agate and carnelian from the cenotaphs of the Emperor and his lamented Queen." More famously, the British ambassador to the Ottoman Empire around the same time removed about half of the surviving Greek sculptures of the Parthenon and hauled them back to the British Museum (the Elgin Marbles are now a source of bitter international contention).

How much cleaner was it back then? If you look closely, you will always find the seed of trespass that led eventually to the entanglement we are dealing with now. An episode comes to mind, the fate of one of the most important archaeological sites in northwest China at the beginning of the 1900s. For China it was the archaeological crime of the century, and it starts like a joke: a Taoist monk runs into a British archaeologist in the desert. But to get the full story, we must go back a few years before this fateful meeting.

It begins with a forgotten library at the edge of the Taklamakan Desert in China, where towers of scrolls once lay heaped upon each other under several centuries of dust. In this collection was the Diamond Sutra, the oldest known printed book in the world (its inscription read May 11, 868, which puts it 587 years earlier than the Gutenberg Bible). There were also the so-called Jesus Sutras, extremely rare texts of Christian teachings introduced to China in the seventh century. There were stacks of Tibetan *pothi*, originally brought from far away and housed by the thousands, along with scrolls from a number of other cultures and a handful of diverse written languages. The scrolls contained legends, ballads, rhymes, medical charts, and rules for debtors—the meticulously detailed record of an earlier civilization. There was even a thousand-year-old etiquette guide that explained the exact words one should use to apologize to a host for drunkenness at a party, and how a host would properly respond to such an apology. This is the kind of collection in situ that archaeologists would die for.

For centuries the collection remained hidden in a cave, and until its final years, only one person knew of its existence, the one who had first found it. A lone monk, he would sit hunched over these manuscripts. By the wobbling flame of a butter lamp he studied languages unremembered, pages of history, military documents, and the painstaking calligraphy of monks and saints who had died many centuries before. Though mostly illiterate, unable to understand all that he was seeing, the monk turned one soft page after the next, enraptured.

The monk's name was Wang Yuanlu. A pious young man

who around 1899 was living at the edge of civilization, he was the keeper of the Caves of the Thousand Buddhas, a site of ruined temples he had stumbled upon in a winter-frozen desert. His self-appointed job was to protect this place.

Yuanlu had come to this remote region of northwest China during his service in the Chinese infantry, when he vowed to become an ascetic in the Taoist tradition. After leaving the military, he found these ruins and dilapidated meditation caves, a perfect place for him to live out his years alone with his bowl and his blanket. But the site proved more significant than he had imagined. Hundreds of chambers and spacious halls had been carved into the bedrock with architectural finesse. The site had been built on a major stop along the Silk Road, the once great trade route between China and the farther domains of Rome and the Middle East. Merchants and travelers received blessings here and gave offerings before setting out across the dangerous Taklamakan Desert, and this was where they stopped on their return to give thanks. By the time Yuanlu arrived, the place had been abandoned for well over a thousand years, evacuated by monks fleeing an imminent invasion. They had left behind ruined temples, buildings made of wood and plaster sagging against each other. Most had collapsed upon themselves, their timbers cocked out of the ground. The ruins and caves went on for a mile, with whole sections burned, posts black and weathered.

With his lamp or perhaps the stub of a candle, Yuanlu would have moved like a firefly through catacomb-like passages housing two thousand derelict statues of bodhisattvas and warrior gods. You can imagine him in one of the larger temples—which had been cut back into bedrock to form a deeply shadowed chamber—pausing and lifting his light beneath a seventy-five-foot-tall Buddha, its enormous hands cupped over his head. All around him were murals, what amounted to about 150,000 square feet of wall-to-wall images—one of the largest painted spaces ever created in the ancient world.

The temples were in bad shape. Centuries of neglect had left entryways choked with rubble and sand drifted six feet deep into unattended rooms. Yuanlu vowed to return at least some of the site to its original glory.

A year after his arrival he was sweeping away sand that had drifted against a wall when he exposed a narrow wooden door. He jimmied it open only to find it bricked up. As he pulled out bricks one by one, light spilled onto a hoard of manuscripts, nearly fifty thousand scrolls and paintings, so many lumped one on another that the ones near the bottom were flattened. The library he discovered had been sealed off since the tenth century.

Believing he had made a great find, Yuanlu removed two of the finest manuscripts and rushed them to the local magistrate, ten miles away in Dunhuang. He was hoping that a decree of preservation would be offered, but the magistrate, unimpressed, pushed the stiffened paper aside. Three years later a new magistrate arrived, and Yuanlu, who had been frequenting the library to pore over texts, convinced him to come see the cave for himself. But the new man simply took a few manuscripts and told Yuanlu to keep an eye on the place. Yuanlu felt his find was more important than that. He packaged up two crates of manuscripts and hauled them 250 miles to a larger government center, the prefecture of Jiuquan, where his find was finally recognized as an important piece of Chinese history. In 1904 Yuanlu finally received an official order to protect the cave, to make sure no unscrupulous travelers made off with this remarkable piece of the past. This was now his job.

. . .

In June of 1906 Aurel Stein, one of the world's greatest archaeological explorers, came riding out of a red-sky windstorm into Kashgar, in Chinese Turkistan. Dust poured from tucks in his tightly folded coat, making him look more like a local Taklamakanchi than a scholar. His square, stern face was powerfully weathered, his cheekbones standing out like polished stones. He kept the small crease of his mouth clamped shut against the wind. Standing a staunch five foot four, Stein was at the midpoint of sixteen years spent mostly in the north of Asia, excavating fortresses and shrines to keep the British Museum well supplied. He was following the route of an ancient pilgrim and scholar named Xuanzang, who in the sixth century had traveled across Asia in a quest for knowledge, stopping at temples and cities that are now in ruins. These ruins were Stein's goldmine, and Xuanzang was his personal saint.

Stein had no wife, no children; his life was the hunt for archaeology. Word had come to him that outside Dunhuang a hidden library had been found among painted caves, and this was his target. He had to hurry to get there. The Germans and French had gotten wind of this, too, and he did not know how close behind they were. After thousands of miles of travel, his caravans floundering through gorges and fifteen-thousand-foot passes, he was not about to surrender this find.

In the cobble-and-adobe town of Kashgar, Stein assembled a caravan of eight fresh camels and a number of horses, and with them set across the Taklamakan, a thousand desolate miles to Dunhuang and the Caves of the Thousand Buddhas. Along the way, he stopped at ancient cities lost in the desert, where he oversaw rapid excavations, a team of hired diggers working under desiccating winds and snow flurries. Spending only a few days at each site, he pushed on toward Dunhuang while sending back trains of camels loaded with crates of artifacts bound for London.

One must wonder if the back of Yuanlu's neck prickled or if his ears burned as Stein approached from the west. The world was being taken apart and put back together in England, and for a man like Stein, that was simply the way things were done. It was a time of immense archaeological wealth and freedom for colonial powers.

If you could choose the course of history for the Caves of the Thousand Buddhas, would you divert Stein with a great Taklamakan dust storm, adding his bones to those of the many who perished along his route, rather than let him at Yuanlu's library?

Before you decide, consider the other half of the equation. Pith-helmeted nimrods and colonial frolickers were not the only people chipping away at global antiquities. Locals were already in on the action, digging and selling. Chinese manuscripts were all the rage during Stein's reign, and the market was being flooded with forgeries. A find like the library cave would have drawn burglars and explorers far less reputable and connected than Stein. Rather than being housed in the British Museum, texts would have been divided countless ways, lost to private collections and obscure places.

Here you have your choice. Does Stein reach the library and take all he can, or do the texts stay with Yuanlu, if only for the moment of his life?

· · ·

On March 12, 1907, Stein came riding into Dunhuang out of an icy spring wind called a *buran*. It was an auspicious day. The town was nearing a revolt as citizens refused to pay

taxes levied by the distant Qing government. The local magistrate was already overwhelmed. When Stein presented his
passport, which incorrectly identified him as "Minister of
Education for Great Britain," the magistrate was quickly
humbled. A visit from such an important man at this far end
of civilization was rare. At the archaeologist's behest he ushered Stein directly to the Caves of the Thousand Buddhas.

Stein and Yuanlu missed each other completely that day.
The monk was walking the streets of Dunhuang with his
bowl seeking alms to help him care for the caves, while Stein
was earnestly hunting his destiny.

Approaching the caves ten miles from town, Stein would
have crossed a dry riverbed beyond which stood a grove
of bare elm and poplar trees. Above them rose a cliff
honeycombed with hundreds of hand-hewn grottoes, great
temples fallen apart. Ratty silk scarves had been left by
pilgrims.

Inside, the site was spectacular, like a dream. Usually
Stein had to dig to find a place like this, but here was this
marvel open to the air: lobed and painted entryways cut into
rock, leading to catacombs of meditation alcoves and massive interior halls, native bedrock carved to simulate classic
architecture, columns, eaves, coffered ceilings. Inside this
magnificent subterranean world all but the floors had been
decorated with murals—winged thunder demons, musi-
cians on clouds, a nine-headed dragon, all rendered with
such detail that the walls would have looked to Stein like
Persian rugs.

When he finally met Yuanlu, Stein was taken aback. The
young monk who approached him was even shorter than he,
his face weathered but somehow soft. Stein's notes and
letters, which had previously focused on artifacts, landscape, and himself, were suddenly busy with descriptions of
his new acquaintance. He referred to Yuanlu as sullen,

frightened, truculent, and anxious. "A very queer person," Stein declared in a letter, "extremely shy and nervous with an occasional expression of cunning which was far from encouraging." Yet in almost the same breath, observing that the monk spent next to nothing on himself but instead put alms directly into the temples, Stein wrote, "I could not help feeling something akin to respect for the queer little figure."

Stein considered offering his host silver for access to this secret library, but he worried the approach would backfire. He dared not even mention that he had heard of the place, for fear that Yuanlu would shut him down.

Stein knew bits of local dialects and various languages spoken in the area, Chinese, Turki, Uyghur, and Wakhi, enough to hire diggers or send out crates. But when it came to delicate negotiations he was plagued by what he called the "eel-like perplexity of Chinese phonetics and the terrible snares of tonic accents so hard for unmusical ears to distinguish." Chiang-ssü-yeh, a Chinese secretary who had accompanied him across the Taklamakan, acted as a translator. At one point Chiang turned to Stein and sagely advised him to "feel his way with prudence and studied slowness." Yuanlu, he felt, was not about to give up an inch of his temples, much less his library.

Yuanlu was hospitable, though. He guided Stein and his translator around without mentioning the library cave. He took them through his restorations, showing off the new gilded woodwork and paint. Stein found Yuanlu's restorations gaudy and overblown, insulting to the finesse of what was there to begin with. But he said none of this to Yuanlu.

Then Stein mentioned Xuanzang, the ancient scholar who was his own saint. Yuanlu's eyes lit up. Stein could have felt the key turning.

Xuanzang was a popular mythological figure among monks in China. His sixth-century quest had been to understand the different ways people worshipped throughout Asia, a journey that took him on a sixteen-year trek, two thousand miles of now-legendary travel. When he finally returned to China he brought a horse train loaded with foreign religious texts—not unlike what Stein expected to find in the library.

Indeed, Yuanlu had a place in his heart for the old pilgrim-scholar Xuanzang. Carefully seizing the moment, Stein explained through his interpreter that he, too, was a devoted follower of Xuanzang, which was quite true. Stein imparted that he had been traveling across the very mountains and deserts Xuanzang had crossed, stopping at the same sanctuaries.

Yuanlu quickly took Stein to see murals of Xuanzang's journeys that he had found within the caves. Painted in the chambers were mythical episodes. In one, a mighty turtle was shown swimming toward Xuanzang and his horse in order to carry them across a raging river. Stein knew the very river. He had crossed it himself, and in its wild waters had nearly lost his own horses and many manuscripts he had already excavated from other sites.

With the seed planted, Stein left his interpreter and Yuanlu to converse without him. That night Chiang returned to his employer's camp and from his voluminous black cloak pulled several manuscripts. He said that Yuanlu had offered them for Stein to study in secrecy, so as not to arouse the suspicions of locals or the guards sent by the magistrate to protect Stein and also keep an eye on him. (At an archaeological site who could trust a foreigner with a caravan of camels at his disposal?) Stein unrolled one of these manuscripts across a table. The paper felt like thin cloth, and on it were slips and dashes of calligraphy from a language he believed to date back to the third century.

In the morning Chiang brought more, including an Indian

sutra translated into Chinese stamped with the inscription of Xuanzang himself. Stein was astonished. These were the old monk's actual translations, his own hand, his very words. Surely this was some sort of omen. In his notes, Stein had more than once pondered the similarities between himself and Xuanzang. He was starting to believe that he was Xuanzang incarnate, sent here to continue the old pilgrim's work of unearthing ancient texts, freeing them from what Stein called their "gloomy bin of centuries."

He went straight to Yuanlu and explained to the young monk that there was no coincidence in their meeting. Xuanzang was calling out across the centuries. It was all happening again, just as it did over a millennium ago. It was again time for the manuscripts to go.

Pale with honor, and probably filled with tickling hesitation, Yuanlu removed the bricks he had used to reseal the door to the library cave. Behind the door Stein found exactly what he had wished for, later writing, "Heaped up in layers, but without any order, there appeared in the dim light of the priest's little lamp a solid mass of manuscript bundles rising to a height of ten feet, and filling, as subsequent measurement showed, close on 500 cubic feet."

After days of sorting through this library to find what he considered the best material, Stein was given leave to take whatever he wished. In gratitude, he paid in silver and quietly loaded his camels with twenty-four crates of manuscripts, and five crates of paintings and embroideries. Roughly a third of the library's contents was now destined for the British Museum. He left Dunhuang with a full caravan.

Stein's appropriation opened the floodgates. Soon after him, the French arrived. Then the Japanese. And then a Russian team. A swaggering collector from Harvard would later arrive and strip murals off the walls to send back to the

United States. In 1909, the Chinese government found out what was going on and issued a decree stating that any remaining texts had to be taken to Beijing, to be kept there by the Ministry of Education. With that, the library cave was cleared down to its floor. A chamber that had been packed nearly to the ceiling for centuries was now vacant. Did Yuanlu's heart break, or was his life's quest fulfilled?

. . .

Stein got away with some of the most spectacular literary finds in the world, the Diamond Sutra and thousands more in his crates. Of course, a world power such as China is now wondering why such a detailed and exhaustive account of its own history reposes in London and elsewhere. In China, Stein has come to be called a "foreign devil." Even Chinese scholars writing dry scientific papers add colorful words like *plunderer* and *thief* when describing Stein's work at Dunhuang. To this day the official Chinese media portrays him as a scoundrel who fooled an impressionable young monk into giving up crucial pieces of national patrimony.

But truth be told, if Stein and his colleagues had not been the first into the library after Yuanlu, there would have been others far less high-minded who would have sold their finds to the highest bidders. The contents of the library cave would have probably been scattered and mostly forgotten. Now they are contained in a handful of well-catalogued museum collections around the world. These incredibly old and otherwise obscure writings are internationally known and studied, their translations readily available online. If the Chinese had taken immediate control of the manuscripts prior to Stein's arrival, their fate might have been far worse. At that point in history the country could barely conserve its own imperial palace, much less a library outside of a frontier town on the verge of rebellion. Not knowing what else to do with them, the government could have either confiscated the manuscripts and lost them to poor storage, or crated them up and dumped them into an unmarked warehouse, never to be seen in any of our lifetimes. Even the final shipment of manuscripts from Dunhuang to Beijing was robbed en route, and portions soon appeared in the private collection of a well-known Chinese bibliophile.

Though Stein is revealed in his notes and journal entries as having been presumptuous and full of hubris, I also see that he was a savior. Sometimes things work out in unexpected ways, a negotiation resulting in what is best for antiquity. Stein and Yuanlu may be called star-crossed partners in crime, but they are also the very reason these ancient manuscripts still exist.

How does one weigh the somewhat necessary emptying of the library cave against the desire for things to remain where they were found? I've come to believe that each circumstance is unique and that there is no generic solution. I would leave relics where they are, yet I would also side with Stein in preserving the past by moving it.

Stein's collection (perhaps more aptly named the Stein and Yuanlu Collection) is now housed in the British Museum. Not on public display, it is held in breathtakingly clean storage. What he boxed up and carried out by camel has since undergone intensive preservation work (including efforts to undo earlier failed attempts at conservation, such as the removal of a damaging backing put on the Diamond Sutra). In Stein's shadow, the new discipline of Dunhuangology sprang up and one of the largest single collaborations of scholars and archaeologists in the world, the International Dunhuang Project, was eventually assembled. The manuscripts have since been studied in excruciating detail, down to the very chemistry of their ink. Given a choice between piecemealing the archive into nothing or this, I choose this. For now.

China will someday want the contents of this library back. No formal petition has been offered, but an official at the Chinese embassy in London recently said, "When the time comes I think the Chinese authorities will request the return of these relics. It's hard to say when that will be. Little by little, we will expect to see the return of items taken from Dunhuang. They should go back to their original place." The British Museum has balked, saying that if they gave these items back, they would open the floodgates for all sorts of collections that would be called into question. But stonewalling by a slowly declining nation in the face of a rising China can suffice only so long.

China is now becoming a major purchasing force in the global antiquities and art market, buying back what was once taken. At a 2010 sale at Christie's in New York, roughly two-thirds of the 611 lots up for auction were acquired by Chinese dealers and collectors. As the *New York Times* arts correspondent Souren Melikian noted, "They bought across the board, in every category, at every financial level." The winds appear to be changing.

It may take another Stein and Yuanlu, another Xuanzang, to loosen this collection from the grip of the British Museum. It would be a beguiling thing if all that was gathered from Yuanlu was returned, the library reinstalled in its cave, the entry sealed with bricks, and dust allowed to drift over the door until we once again forget what was there and why.

CHAPTER 8

THE CHOSEN ONES

The role of archaeologist has changed over the years. If Aurel Stein had tried to get away with his acquisitions in the twenty-first century, he would simply have been arrested.

Randall McGuire, a vocal researcher from Binghamton University in New York, has written, "At the dawn of the twenty-first century ethics in archaeology are not simple. They are very complex, conflicted, and confusing. Today, ethical questions and dilemmas are more about relations among people than about things." McGuire wrote about performing fieldwork in rural northern Mexico, where locals were convinced he was looking for treasure. They wondered why else a man and his crew would toil under the summer sun all day. At one point, a little boy ran up to McGuire asking if he was from the United States. McGuire said yes, and the boy asked if he was looking for gold and silver. McGuire shook his head no and began explaining what archaeologists really do, how they are picking up specimens to better understand what happened in the past. Before he could finish, however, the boy ran off, unconvinced.

Sensing unrest and misunderstanding, McGuire decided to hold a town meeting. He explained to about a hundred people that he was there with support from the National Geographic Society, his task being to study the remains of ancient maize farmers and shell-jewelry makers. He promised that he was taking nothing of value from them, no gold or silver. Many remained unconvinced. McGuire eventually shrugged off this misunderstanding as a sort of entrenched local mistrust, but what he failed to realize was that the locals were right. He was indeed looking for treasure, only they could not imagine that it resided in the bits and pieces he was picking up.

Like so many others, archaeologists have proclaimed themselves as rightful stewards and recipients of the past. And also like so many others, they value their treasures for unique reasons. It used to be more about big finds, statues and manuscripts. Now it is about everything. Information is treasure—not the object alone, but the way it fits into the larger fabric of its context. If it is touched by someone else (even another archaeologist of less propriety), if it is moved, altered, taken, or destroyed, the larger picture becomes unrecoverable. Archaeologists rely on eighth-inch strata, reflections of X-rays, and the arrangement of isotopes. Was the artifact found in a ceremonial setting, a kitchen, or a grave? Was it left randomly along a trail or placed in a special room? If we had access to the original library at the Caves of the Thousand Buddhas, it would now take years to unload the room—the position of every manuscript taken into account, layers of time added up, dust analyzed for its properties. Not exactly Stein's quick dash. Science has become ever more delicate, requiring virgin context, which puts archaeologists at extreme odds with modern collectors who are not so concerned with provenance, or pothunters who dig at will.

Archaeologists have mounted an unflagging offensive against looters, collectors, and anyone else on what is seen as "that side of the fence." Many researchers refuse to consider using artifacts or collections that did not benefit from methodical, scientific study. The notoriously bad provenance of sellable artifacts is equated with bad science, and any involvement with it (such as helping date or even price a dubious piece as Roxanna Brown did) is seen as reinforcing a market that wrecks the archaeological record. Many of the leading voices in archaeology decree that even communicating with collectors or dealers is a sin. The illicit hunt for fresh antiquities is the number one reason that archaeological sites around the world look as if they've been hit with a locustlike plague of looters, and archaeologists often see themselves as a force working against this destruction.

In 2000, the Society for American Archaeology (SAA) named stewardship as the first priority of any professional archaeologist. As SAA official ethics now state, "Stewards are both caretakers of and advocates for the archaeological record for the benefit of all people; as they investigate and interpret the record, they should use the specialized knowledge they gain to promote understanding and support for its long-term preservation."

But one must ask, preservation by and for whom? The idea of stewardship in scientific circles is nothing new, and it has been employed in the past with shameful results. In the late 1800s and early 1900s scientists went out like armies to "save" Native America from perishing. They believed cultural memory would soon wink out as tribes and clans fell to Manifest Destiny. Saving it meant preserving artifacts and oral histories for later study, and the work was done with the best of intentions. Ceremonial chambers still in use were gutted of objects, as if snatching crosses, candles, and vestments from a church. Totem poles came down. Moccasins and sandals were packed into boxes. These things were bought for a song, paid for with tobacco, window glass, lumber, or a handful of dollars. George Peabody, founder of the Peabody Museum at Harvard, one of the greatest purely ethnographic museums in the world, wrote in 1866 that "in view of the gradual obliteration or destruction of the works and remains of the ancient races of this continent, the labor of exploration and collection [should] be commenced at as early a day as practicable." The sentiment was shared around the world, and it targeted many cultures. Pygmies and yak herders and Aborigines were all thought to be inevitable casualties of progress. On their way out of existence they were to leave their things at the door, to be taken care of by stewards.

No one counted on population rebounds and crowded reservations, Indian colleges and casinos. No one thought indigenous cultures would survive to start demanding their things back, for example Tasmanian Aborigines pressuring European museums for the return of "historical ancestors," and Australian Aborigines getting back the head of one of their leaders that had been stewarded in London as an anthropological curiosity. Native Americans gained the political foothold to markedly change laws governing archaeology in the United States. When they say they want something returned, it is no longer considered idle talk. After the 1990 passage of NAGPRA, museums in the United States were legally mandated to prepare all qualifying Indian remains and sacred objects for repatriation. What the tribes want—within the letter of the law—they come and get. (In the case of artifacts that have been bathed in poisons to prevent their decay, they got more than they bargained for.)

Though institutions assume public relations smiles about the matter, they have been strained by the demands of NAGPRA. Often understaffed, they receive little or no additional funding to cover the workload, while the backlash has denied archaeologists permission to analyze human remains they dug themselves, battling over access to the likes of Washington State's Kennewick Man with all the legal force they can muster. One archaeologist who declined to be named confided in me, "NAGPRA? It's just a big pain in the ass."

Considering the inconstancy of cultural mandates and different interpretations from within the science, what does *stewardship* even mean? Archaeologists and anthropologists relying on artifacts are, in fact, users as much as they are stewards. They employ the archaeological record for their own ends, reconstructing the past in a rational, institutional manner. If an artifact is to be dug out of the ground, I would want to see it in an archaeologist's hands. What with their careful observation and skills of long-term preservation, they are a far cry from pothunters. But since archaeologists hold themselves up as self-selected stewards, they invite close scrutiny.

·   ·   ·

A rooster tail of dust came up from a dirt road along the ochre margins of the Painted Desert, about forty miles east of Show Low, Arizona. Near the road's end, a truck stopped at a bald promontory. Six diggers got out. Loaded down with shovels, hammers, and toolboxes, they trudged up a trail with the resolve of firefighters. At the top, they set down their things at the edge of a settlement that had been buried for eight hundred years, a circular great kiva with a cluster of residences built off to one side. The crew had come to empty a portion of this site, something they had been working on for weeks. Tarps were yanked off, ballast rocks rolled out of the way, and they went straight to work. Down on their knees, they had a long way to go and a short season to get there. They had come from the University of Arizona in Tucson to study ancient settlement patterns, and what they were digging would offer an even finer-grained lens through which to view the people who had lived on this spot on the map.

As the day's heat came on across a scorched landscape, dust devils began stirring. One whipped around the edge of a trench, a whirling pipe of fine sand that caused the woman at the bottom, an undergrad, to look up from her small task in the hard-packed earth. She wiped sweat and dirt from under the rim of her sunglasses. The dust devil crossed the excavation, then fanned into the air, gone. The woman scanned the horizon—a yellow-colored land rolling into the distance—and then fell again to her assignment.

"What's that?" I asked, crouched at the edge of her trench.

Troweling around a circle, she said, "The mouth of a corrugated jar."

"Intact?" I asked.

"It's got some cracks in it. Looks like it's shattered. But I'll bet it's all here."

She worked at the jar like a sculptor, brushing and carving, her motions delicately expressing the vessel's gray curves. I watched carefully, excited just like her to see another patch of jar that had not been touched by daylight since it was buried centuries ago. As British archaeologist Michael Shanks once described, "Excavation is striptease. The layers are peeled off slowly; eyes of intent scrutiny. The pleasure is in seeing more, but it lies also in the edges: the edge of a stocking-top and thigh. There is the allure of transgression—the margin of decorum and lewdness, modesty and display." Indeed, like every excavation I have ever attended, this one was tinged with a little impropriety—an absolutely vulnerable thing very intentionally being revealed by an outsider—yet it happened with an extreme delicacy that made it seem somehow excusable, not as rough and raunchy as the actions of a pothunter, who could have this thing dug up in less than a minute. (The jar being exposed today was a ceramic type Earl Shumway once said he would have tossed just to watch it smash.)

The dig boss opened a file box, pulled out folders, and marched around checking off his lists while I watched the gray jar slowly emerge. It was being done right, the entire trench taken down like layers sliced off a cake, a purely scientific approach with a full record made of every eighth of an inch. As the PhD overseeing the project told me, the work is state of the art, every imaginable measurement accounted for, every object removed (along with samples of the dirt and the pollens in them). They were not taking the entire site, only a handful of trenches, like a crossword puzzle pulled from the ground.

What was happening here was completely legal, ordained by government minions. There was no fear of federal agents, and no motion detectors or hidden cameras to signal a trespass.

The first piece of the jar came loose, and the woman drew it out of its setting.

"Here," she said, passing the piece up to me.

It was an eggshell curve about half the size of my palm, slightly blackened on the outside from cook fires, caked on the inside with soil; perhaps there might have been a bit of cornmeal preserved in its pores. I held it up between thumb and forefinger, thinking this was a remarkable moment: a vessel that had sat inert for centuries was suddenly put in motion, its round shape coming apart for the first time. This kind of thing becomes an addiction. Some archaeologists I know—a minority—have trouble staying within strict excavation boundaries. They want to follow a pottery cluster they find, or a lens of charcoal and fire ash, which leaves them slicing off extra layers of earth to see what is behind the curtain. These kinds of diggers are referred to as "deep sweepers," and it is not a term of endearment. Archaeology is called a discipline for a reason. You stick to your job.

That summer I was going from dig to dig, hopscotching

around the Southwest to get a taste of different excavations. I visited the Homol'ovi Project near Winslow where for a couple of days I helped excavate in a fierce desert wind, and then refreshed myself at the U of A field camp up in the cool, piney woods above the Mogollon Rim. From there I spent another several days on a tenth-century great-house excavation in the Four Corners, unearthing a chamber under the big sky.

I was an archaeology groupie. Summers before, I had worked as a base camp cook for museum excavations in Colorado. I would do anything to get close to these peepholes that were being dug in time. It was, indeed, a privilege. Even if I only excavated mouse bones, potsherds, and horizons of fine, gray dust, the sense of revelation springing out of the ground was well worth it. (Not to mention enthusiastic camps awash in evening talk about ancient wars and migrations. And, of course, there were nights spent in poorly lit bars where excavators were far more raucous than the usual ranchers and drunks.) I have secretly wished to be an archaeologist myself, but I do not have the patience for the scientific tedium involved, which would test model-ship builders. Though digging with them felt like a free pass to get underground, afterward I would scrub my hands hard with water, as if trying to wash off blood.

The woman in the trench asked if I would start a bag for her. I snapped open a brown-paper lunch sack and slid the sherd inside.

Though most of the site was being left untouched, ostensibly for future scholars with better tools, these trenches in particular were to be emptied down to the last speck. The sterile dirt that remained was then to be poured back in to fill the trenches. Because no one knew what crucial piece of data might be revealed later in the lab, what argument might hinge on the most meager find, all specimens were going to the university.

Archaeology is like getting into people's closets, or finding what is lost under the couch, all the dirty little secrets. What hammers did ancient people use, what soup bowls and fire starters? Where did they give birth, and in what holes did they shit (entire master's degrees are spent on desiccated chubs of ancient human feces). Everything must be known, down to nips of charcoal, strands of old cloth, and gnawed rat bones. From these, the past is reconstructed, as if to remind us in agonizing detail that we are not the only people who ever lived.

There is a glitch, though. Much of what has been dug remains undeciphered and unreconstructed. Excavation spoils are piling up. Every major public repository in Arizona will have topped out in five to ten years, a problem faced by institutions across the country and around the world, yet more keeps coming in as cardboard boxes and bags of specimens heap onto each other in storage.

Smaller collections across the country can hardly afford to curate what has already been delivered. The U.S. Army Corps of Engineers oversees 50,000 cubic feet of artifacts from field recoveries, and three-quarters of this collection is improperly stored, most of it steadily deteriorating. It would take $20 million to put it in order. One university kept an annex of anthropological collections in a two-bay car wash, a triage location that was the only place they could find. A windstorm blew the roof off and in came the weather, damaging much of the collection.

Speaking to what is being called a "curation crisis," Bob Sonderman, a senior staff archaeologist with the National Park Service, complained of too many chicken bones and fire-cracked rocks he and his colleagues are charged to preserve.

He said, "In a climate where space is equated with money, archaeologists must face the hard reality that we simply can't keep everything."

In the United States, we now have over 200 million individually catalogued objects in the public trust. In addition, there are 2.6 million cubic feet of artifacts stored in bulk whose individual pieces have yet to be catalogued, which comes out to about 1,300 semi truckloads of potsherds, beads, bones, shells, feathers, and buttons. This is what institutional obsession looks like. When you wander through repositories with tens of thousands of vessels indefinitely awaiting analysis, you get a picture of what archaeology has truly created: not a diorama of the past, but a diorama of ourselves. It is our own desire for the past stacking on itself.

Mark Varien, a thoughtful scholar of the Southwest, once said that the science is an effort in preservation, both of the object and of antiquity itself. Archaeology must be either saved in the ground or collected in a professional manner, or else it is lost to us. Varien believes in the authenticity of touch. He heads a research center that frequently brings the public to work at sites, which is where he sees people truly connecting with the past. He told me, "Increasing population, ongoing development, and the forces of nature all destroy parts of the archaeological record every day. Think about the world 100 years from now, 1,000 years from now, and tens of thousands of years from now. Imperfect as it may be, the record of human occupation on the planet, as preserved through archaeological documentation, is important for understanding human behavior now and in the future."

For Varien, as for most archaeologists, sites are a nonrenewable resource, the legacy of human occupation on this planet that, once taken from the ground, is forever changed. He calls his science imperfect, admitting it actually destroys the in-the-ground record by removing it, something pothunters are frequently accused of. "But we document what we find," he emphasizes. "Through this documentation what has been destroyed is preserved, hopefully in perpetuity."

Frederick Matthew Wiseman, an author, archaeologist, and member of the Abenaki Tribal Council in Vermont, sees this sort of preservation as a one-way street. An artifact is taken from its source and carried up through a chain of hands, where it ultimately enriches a community far from the source, a community he sees as the "ultimate consumer." But what about back at the source? Wiseman writes that "viewed from the perspective of the elder who has lost legal control of her life story, the backfilled hole that was once a site, or the plant crucified on acid-free paper in some paradichlorobenzined herbarium cabinet, this may seem exploitive to say the least."

The federal field archaeologist Glade Hadden once told me it is "an act of silliness" when archaeologists remove artifacts. "I don't take things anymore unless I have to, if it's at obvious risk of being destroyed," he explained. "The argument 'if we don't take it somebody else will' doesn't work for me. If you're really a scientist, why would you need to possess the object itself? It's just an object. It's just stuff. For what archaeologists purport themselves to be, all they really need is context. After that you're just a collector."

. . .

The crew took a break for lunch at the edge of the dig site, rifling through a bag of chips and eating sandwiches. Before us lay the theater of northeast Arizona, a parched expanse capped by the enormous blue shell of the sky. We talked about digging and taking, and when I asked, some of the students admitted feeling a twinge of violation in their work.

Why them? they asked. Why now? Why should anyone have the right or not to excavate someone else's history? I ventured a story and told them about the pot I once returned to the wilderness. (I carefully left out the part about how it came into my possession, a difficult omission, for fear they might turn on me.) To my surprise, they enjoyed the story. It seemed to reflect their own ambivalence about removing artifacts in the first place. "It's a good question," the dig boss said. "Do we really need all of this?" Another chimed in, "It is kind of strange what we're all doing out here digging up dead people's things."

Then, nobody said anything. We looked across the view, listened to the sky.

As we returned to the trenches, people taking positions on hands and knees, I thought back to something I read from Charles Bowden, a dry and brilliant desert writer. While wandering in intense sunlight, surrounded by the remains of the dead, he said that a set of rules came to him, rules that define what we must contend with as we explore this land. They are:

"1. You are in the right place.
2. You do not belong here.
3. Deal with this fact.
4. Time's up."

. . .

Archaeology is one of the younger core disciplines, dating back to the late 1800s (although some argue that it goes back to the likes of the caliph al-Mamun, a ninth-century Arabian scholar and philosopher who oversaw crews tunneling into the Great Pyramid of Giza and was incidentally frustrated to find he was not the first, that the tomb had already been emptied).

In 1891, just before Stein's journeys along the Silk Road, a young Swedish scholar named Gustaf Nordenskiöld came to the Southwest to seek his scientific fortune, and he has been credited with laying the foundation for North American archaeology here. Born to a family of Nordic scientists and adventurers, son of famed polar explorer Adolf Erik Nordenskiöld, he was expected to do great things. By his early twenties he had already ventured to the Arctic and there collected plant fossils that he proudly carried back to the Swedish Museum of Natural History. Now he needed something more substantial to make a name for himself, a find of dramatic and personal merit. Racked as he was by tubercular coughing and terrible night chills, he found the aridity of southwest Colorado a haven. Here he donned a cowboy hat and posed in front of a camera, his fists planted on his hips, his hat brim tipped as if he thought himself Jesse James.

Nordenskiöld soon met the Wetherill brothers, ranchers who had been publicizing their discovery of mysterious cliff dwellings hidden deep within a place called Mesa Verde. At Nordenskiöld's behest they saddled horses and took him to the edge of a precipice where he looked down on a palace of ruins, its towers and rooms half standing, circular ceremonial chambers gaping under collapsed ceilings, property of no one, exactly what an intrepid young explorer would have dreamed of. These were the remains of a cultural zenith in the ancient Southwest, a time of high Anasazi architecture and refined ceramic production. The brothers said the mesa was riddled with such places, each ruin concealing hordes of artifacts inside this canyon-cut mesa. Though his background was in geology and chemistry, Nordenskiöld's skills could be applied equally to what was then the fledgling discipline of archaeology. Back then, science was science.

Nordenskiöld announced his plans to assemble a crew

and perform excavations to study this crumbled and virtually unknown civilization. He would go on to publish the first archaeological treatise in North America, *The Cliff Dwellers of the Mesa Verde, Southwestern Colorado: Their Pottery and Implements.*

The Wetherill brothers had already been eagerly exploring the mesa, digging and collecting in a fashion that would be considered reckless by today's standards. They showed Nordenskiöld where he would find the best artifacts, teaching him how to spot prehistoric graves under rubble and dust that were often rich with pre-Columbian offerings. In turn, Nordenskiöld impressed upon the brothers the need for methodical techniques in their digging, cross-sections and layers of superposition, a newfound scientific discernment that would lay the foundation for future researchers. The Wetherills took quickly to his nuanced work, and together they dug the hearts out of several ruins, pulling up skeletons, necklaces, painted pots, and woven sandals. Soon seventeen crates were packed tight with artifacts and reams of notes, the finest singular haul ever to leave Mesa Verde.

In town, though, there were rumblings. Locals did not like what was happening. The cliff dwellings seemed destined to become one of the country's first archaeological theme parks, if not a source for artifact sales, and no sickly Swede was going to hinder their gravy train. Letters calling Nordenskiöld a thief began to appear in local newspapers as no-trespassing posters went up, his name in bold letters. Who was this man, this baron they called him, who came from another country and took whatever he wished? Granted, the same could be asked of them, the mostly Anglo settlers who had no direct kinship with these ruins. But as far as they were concerned it was finders keepers, and this early archaeologist was a latecomer. As wanted posters of Nordenskiöld started going up, the Denver & Rio Grande

Railroad halted his outgoing shipments of artifacts bound for Sweden. On a September night in Durango, Colorado, a mob gathered outside the Strater Hotel, where he was staying.

At midnight a U.S. marshal with a writ of trespass in his hand banged on his door. Nordenskiöld was put under house arrest, the bail set at a punishing $1,000. Ordered not to leave the hotel, Nordenskiöld remained in his room, waiting for his future to unfold.

Top levels of both the U.S. and Swedish governments got involved as Nordenskiöld became a matter of global diplomacy. The U.S. attorney general was finally forced to admit that there was no law at the time preventing a man from taking whatever piece of archaeology he found. Nordenskiöld and his artifacts were allowed to leave. (You can visit the largest Mesa Verde collection outside the United States at the National Museum of Finland in Helsinki, where Nordenskiöld's artifacts are now held.)

Nordenskiöld went into the Southwest thinking himself a scientific hero and barely made it out with his skin. What is legal, allowable, or even ethical changes very quickly, and this reality has continued well after Nordenskiöld's time.

Considering their historic track record, it is no small irony that archaeologists have become so vocal in their opposition to privateers taking artifacts. Attempting to separate themselves from their treasure-hunting origins going back before Nordenskiöld and Stein, they have spruced up their profession with rigorous methodology, focusing on comparative studies and literature reviews more than on straightforward excavations. The science is steadily becoming more about ideas than about things. Many practitioners have made themselves ethically untouchable, writing sanctimonious commentaries about what is right and wrong.

Furthermore, academic fieldwork is more frequently

turning to surface surveys and electronic imaging that can see into buried sites without digging. Fieldworkers may have ultrasonic sensors that automatically map the position, shape, size, and orientation of artifacts in situ, so they do not have to be excavated by hand. It would seem this method moves toward solving many ethical dilemmas of archaeology, but is taking a hands-off approach really the answer for a science born of touching?

Replacing old-fashioned field knowledge with a heavy reliance on technology and floating data may someday be branded a mistake. Subtle relationships, the way the sound of a scraping metal trowel changes when you move out of dirt and into adobe, are lost when you stop digging. No longer will you look up from a half-excavated jar to study the horizon, assimilating an awareness of where you are that no chart or instrument can ever reveal. If archaeology becomes nothing but remote sensing, it risks losing what the discipline tries to forge in the first place, a physical connection to the memory of ancient people. In her alluring book *A Natural History of the Senses*, Diane Ackerman wrote, "There is no way in which to understand the world without first detecting it through the radar-net of our senses." Sense is what gave birth to this science, the act of reaching to the ground and picking up an arrowhead, wondering *Who left this here?*

I once knew an archaeologist named Bruce Anderson who headed digs and surveys for the government across the Southwest in the 1970s and '80s, an era that even now is considered old-school and thought by some to be backward in not conforming to modern techniques. Anderson was the classic field man: bristling mustache, cussing western drawl, a favorite wood-handled trowel. A decade after he retired from digging he pulled his trowel out of a storage box to show me. Its steel blade had originally been as long as his hand, but he had worn it down so short you couldn't use it to flip an egg.

"Now, there's some digging," Anderson had said proudly.

Anderson's work fills volumes. The archaeologists he trained are still awed by his knowledge, his tenacity, even his irreverence. (Out surveying in the desert summer, he would pause to say, "It's hotter than a fresh-fucked fox in a forest fire.") Though Anderson was exhaustive with his documentation, he was likely to spit on academia for its procedural smugness. He wondered how archaeologists could expect the public to appreciate and preserve these things when they were described as little more than sterile scientific commodities.

Anderson personifies the link between the early days of enthusiastic digging and the upright professionalism of the current discipline. When, in the winter of 2008, he was felled by a stroke, I stayed with him, fetching water and coffee. One morning in the dark before dawn, we sat in his living room, me on his couch, he in his cat-scratched lounger. He said he thought archaeologists were turning overly political and embarrassingly self-righteous. He found their papers increasingly arcane, nearly impossible even for him to decipher. They seemed to be saying that archaeology is not about treasure hunting but about the meticulous assembly of data, a vacuum sweeping the countryside for information. He said they were forgetting the reason for archaeology in the first place.

What is that reason?

"We wanted to find out what was in the ground, what cultural groups were physically made of," he said. "When we were digging there wasn't a question about what we were doing. And we didn't have to put on these goddamned airs."

Only weeks before his death Anderson leaned over to me and said, "Fuck 'em."

. . .

Bruce Anderson would have liked this dig on the hill, sun past high noon, dust devils kicking around the site. This is archaeology at its unapologetic heart: we were in the very place where antiquities originated, our lips cracked with the same dust that blanketed an early civilization. This is what the science has long stood for, a cluster of students at the end of a dirt road digging in the heat. It is what collectors rarely get: real, live context.

The undergrad folded her body around what was left of the jar. Pieces kept coming up to me, and I gladly kept sliding them into their sack. Over the hours, I moved around the trench following the shade of my hat brim, and though the work was slow, I remained attentive to every new scrape, leaning in closer to watch her pry off chunks of dirt revealing a new surface. I felt grateful for her patience and doctoring care. This way of working engages far more of the "radar-net of our senses" than the blast holes I have seen elsewhere.

Of all the removers vying for the past, archaeologists are the ones I tend to side with. If an artifact has to be taken, these people keep the most accurate connection with the ground through their documentation. But as gingerly as they operate, this taking of artifacts brings to mind the iconic movie scene where a dusty adventurer carefully weighs out a bag of sand, then switches it with a golden idol. The character's cry — "That belongs in a museum!" — rings out through the science, leaving sand where there was once a key piece of history. Things have been moved, changed, and with them their stories have invariably been reshaped. It is Heisenberg's uncertainty principle applied to archaeology: you can't touch old things without changing them. Robert Layton and Gillian Wallace, two scholars in the field from the UK, wrote,

"Indeed, even when documented, a piece of material is subject to new and different labels when it is placed in an archaeological display."

I noticed a woman creeping toward me, moving along the trench on her hands and knees at an almost imperceptible pace. Her subject was a tree root as thick as her forearm. It grew from an emaciated juniper on the side of the hill, an apocalyptic bonsai, and it had broken into the buried settlement by following a moisture gradient along the floor. The root had met the jar and wrapped around it like a tentacle.

The woman digging the root finally met up with the woman digging the jar. Together they divulged an underground affair. Seeking anchorage, the root had slowly encircled the vessel and then in black silence crushed it.

When the last piece of jar came out, the root described a perfect, ghostly hole. It was the only remaining evidence of what had happened here. The jar-digger kept scritching at the soil with her trowel, on her way down to the next level and not looking back. The root-digger went to her pail and pulled out a hacksaw. What was she doing with *that*? I watched her take it over to the root and with ten swift strokes cut the thing out of the trench and throw it over the side. I was aghast. I tend to obsess inappropriately about things like this, so I tried not to say anything. God forbid I should make a fool of myself in front of professional scientists, saying, *They're in love, the root and the jar, can't you see?*

CHAPTER 9

~~~~~~~~~~~~~~~

SALVAGE ARCHAEOLOGY

It is a job. Workers go out and dig. They pull up every artifact they find. Perfectly legal and not entirely academic, it
is a workingman's science. Plats and blueprints tell where to
excavate. Practitioners are known as "salvage" or "rescue"
archaeologists. In informal circles, they call themselves
"shovel bums," toiling through cities and along pipelines,
where they remove all pertinent archaeology in the way of
development.

There is a growing demand for this particular brand of
archaeologist. Backhoes are digging up slave cemeteries and
ancient pagodas, forcing cities to cough up their dead, and
somebody has to deal with it. Roman burials are cropping
up in London while archaeologists in downtown Miami
ponder a circle of postholes that were cut into bedrock a
couple of thousand years ago, doing so on behalf of a frustrated developer who has been planning luxury condomini-
ums for this spot. After thousands of years of traffic, a
marketplace in Cairo recently revealed a temple containing
a four-ton statue of Ramses II that had been right under
people's feet. Even in the slums of Mexico City, pieces of the
fallen Aztec Empire keep showing up. In 2006, construction
work exposed a thirteen-ton stone carving of an earth

goddess, and when salvage archaeologists went in they discovered it was topping the tomb of an Aztec emperor. This could be the biggest discovery in Mexican history, as they dig through the city's wet, mucky foundations to find it.

Salvage archaeology tends to be inglorious. Big finds are uncommon. Mostly, it consists of bones, charcoal, and chipped stone. Business is usually quick and dirty, and it happens behind construction fences, and in many parts of the world it constitutes 90 percent of active digs and discoveries. It is the largest employer of those graduating with degrees in archaeology. Academics do not overtly frown on this profession; many just consider it a step down from the clean, purely scientific work conducted by universities. Put bluntly, it is paid labor.

Tom Wright, a friend and longtime salvager, says, "Most cultural resource management firms do perfectly good work, but they are the McDonald's of the scientific world. They churn out the product, it passes the necessary standards, and the customers get what they want at a reasonable price. The burger-flippers stay gainfully employed doing honest work, and there's room for advancement, into management and beyond, if they have the ambition and the talent. It's got nothing to do with the food, though, and anyone who makes that mistake is in for a rude surprise."

Wright lives in Phoenix, and by his early fifties he had worked the gamut, from an Indian tribe to a global consulting company to a tiny firm operating out of a suburban duplex. He says that, depending on the employer, salvage work often gets reduced to three simple goals: do your fieldwork quickly, hack out a bare minimum of reporting, and move on to the next project. Rarely is there the incremental progress and contemplative tedium of university digs. Companies may be breathing down your neck. At one point Wright found himself arguing with one of his managers, trying to convince him that a site was significant enough to warrant preservation. The manager told Wright to keep his opinions to himself, and the site was soon taken out by bulldozers. Along with pothunters, dealers, and academic archaeologists, these are the next layer of people who are busy removing the past from the ground.

"There is no pressure to do poor work per se," Wright says, "but plenty of pressure to avoid lingering over things that don't contribute directly to the cash flow."

Still, I have never met a salvage archaeologist not enthralled by what is in the ground. For them, it *is* about the food. They want to know what is down there. The past ten years of accelerated development in Phoenix has added more to the archaeological record than the entire previous century. In the back room of a consulting company, Wright once showed me a broad-hipped jar freshly unearthed from an empty lot in his city. It was still crusted with dirt and root scars. The cremated remains of a pre-Columbian individual were packed inside, and he was preparing the jar for repatriation to a local tribe, as is done with all prehistoric human remains found in Phoenix.

"No brushing the dirt off to see if there are paintings, no removal of the contents," Wright explained. "We will catalogue this, study it for a bit, then give it to the tribe."

The jar had come from just two feet under the surface where a new apartment complex was going in. Before his excavation, transients had been sleeping on the lot amid broken bottles, and he marveled at how so few would ever guess what lay beneath them. Holding the jar as if it were a skull, fingers lacing its underside, Wright handed it to me very carefully. He did not give me its weight until his fingers met mine. It was at that moment that I realized the simple utility involved in bringing up the past, and how understated and heartfelt it can be, a tender recovery.

. . .

I once spoke to a developer who was in the process of bull-dozing a pre-Columbian settlement for a housing project at the edge of Phoenix. He was not a bad man. He hired a respectable firm, made sure that graves were emptied and skeletons and funerary offerings shipped back to local Indian tribes before going ahead with the project. I found his office attractively decorated with ancient ceramics from previous digs, mostly pieces from the early Hohokam culture. He obviously had an appreciation for history. I asked how it felt to permanently remove a large archaeological site from the face of the earth, and he responded, "Tell me a place you can dig in the valley without hitting something Hohokam."

He had me there. You would have to build this city on stilts if you wanted archaeology to endure in situ. Remains tend to lie two inches to a few feet under the surface all across Phoenix: burials, kitchen hearths, and Mesoameri-can-style ball courts.

On a hot late-spring afternoon I stopped to watch an urban parking lot being destroyed near the heart of Phoenix to make way for a new light-rail station. When the project had run into human remains, the URS Corporation, one of the largest engineering design firms in the world, had been called in with its troops of salvage archaeologists. A surpris-ing number of prehistoric burials started coming up, which halted the project at astronomical costs to developers. This site was significant enough that the station was pushed back month after month as more discoveries kept popping up.

The crew chief walked me through a field of tanned shoulders and T-shirts, day labor scratching out potsherds and slivers of bone. Wearing jeans, clipboard in hand, tape measure on his belt, the crew chief told me they had so far found the graves of 182 individuals (plus three intentionally buried dogs). Everything dated to around the fifteenth century, a time when Hohokam society was falling apart. Burdened by overpopulation, the land overfarmed and salinated, the Hohokam had been hit with a deadly knockout punch of drought followed by floods that sent them over the edge. Most of the burials found here were women and children, a sign that things had gone terribly awry.

The crew chief introduced me to one of his diggers, a woman named Pam Cox, who took a break to talk. Perched on the tailgate of her truck, she lit a cigarette and pointed to where a bulldozer was now working, telling me they had found the burial of a young mother there, alongside the remains of a fetus, a clutch of bones small as a rabbit's. She said it looked like a miscarriage.

"That's probably how she died, in childbirth," Cox said, her eyes hidden behind sunglasses. "They buried her with her unborn child."

She took a drag on her cigarette and looked at me until I understood how much precious study she had given to this particular grave before a massive steel blade ground through it.

Cox was a mother in her thirties, and she took this work very seriously. I appreciated her forthright attitude. She gestured across the dig, mentioning a little girl that they found buried by herself, shell bracelets shingled up her left arm and all around her caches of pots, pendants, carved fetishes, and a pretty necklace made of 185 polished shell beads. It was one of the richest burials at the site. They called her "the princess," not because of any known social hierarchy, but a name for a girl who had probably been adored. Nicknames are frowned on in a profession that prefers numbers, but as Cox knew, this girl had never been a number. Why should she be one now?

"Over there was a teenager," Cox said, pointing out past a dirt pile. "Extreme case of scoliosis. Her spine looked like this." She traced a big question mark in the air. Cox pulled a folder and opened it in her lap, showing me a diagram she had drawn of the burial. She'd rendered the skeleton in detail, ribs bent inward, each one biologically distorted in its own way. In life, the young woman's chest must have looked crushed as she hobbled through this village, her back crooked under a woven shawl. Cox said the deformities were so great she could not have put much work into the community and certainly could not have survived on her own. She had to have been cared for.

"It wasn't a poor burial either," Cox remarked. "People came out for her. She had six complete vessels and a duck effigy."

"She must have been very loved," I said. I felt as if I were consoling someone at a funeral.

Cox nodded.

The way she spoke, so simply, got to the heart of the matter: nobody owns these remains. They belong to the people who died, who deserve at least human respect as they are being cleared away for a new civilization. We do not possess them. We merely participate with them.

In his essay on whether we can actually harm the dead, Geoffrey Scarre of the Department of Philosophy at the University of Durham, England, wrote, "Whilst a bone may be no more animate than a stone, it is the relic of a man or woman who once thought and felt, was happy and sad, loved and feared as we do. To disinter or disturb it, or to subject it to chemical or physical analysis, is to take a liberty—not with the thing itself but with the person to whom it once belonged." Yet here, it was a necessity. Cox had to personally figure out how this liberty was to be taken. Objectivity is prized in professional archaeology, but how could she not imagine how each death came to this place; the tears, the clenched jaw as another beloved sister, daughter, wife went into the ground.

I asked Cox how many individuals she herself had excavated from this site, and she counted in her head, then said around a hundred.

The crew chief was listening. He pointed out, "We have her do most of the skeletons."

I looked at Cox. She looked away. I asked her, "Do you have some special qualification?"

"No," Cox answered, not looking at me.

"Why you, then?"

She glanced across mounds dug up around us, trying to avoid the question.

"Tell him," the crew chief urged.

She looked at him, then me. I sensed it was none of my business.

"Tell him," he said again. "Tell him why."

She considered my face for a moment.

"I cry the whole time," she finally said.

With that, she stubbed her cigarette on the tailgate and went back to work.

She was the chosen gravedigger because she grieved. I was speechless, watching her snap up a dustpan and a broom—the tools of the trade to get the dead out of our way.

Part Three

WHERE ARTIFACTS END UP

CHAPTER 10

THE GOLDEN JAR

Everything that is removed goes somewhere, pauses briefly in a pocket or on a shelf. Pieces end up in museums or private collections, or they are reburied in very private repatriation ceremonies. They are destroyed by fires or wars, or they vanish into garages and rented storage containers. The only known surviving statue by the Greek sculptor Praxiteles was, according to its most recent paperwork, found a decade ago in a rubbish pile on a German estate. Apparently it once stood in an immaculate garden, but the vicissitudes of decades left the place in ruins. This famous life-size rendering of Apollo the Lizard Slayer — seen and commented upon by Pliny the Elder in the first century — was discovered in pieces. Once its value was ascertained, it sailed from dealer to dealer until it was purchased by Hicham Aboutaam, who turned it around to the Cleveland Art Museum, whereupon both Italy and Greece immediately demanded its return. If the provenance for this statue is accurate, this last surviving work of the most celebrated of ancient sculptors could have just as easily been hauled to a dump. Would that have been such an unfortunate end? One could imagine that thousands of years from now, if such a people exist, they might dig in our dumps to discover sculptures for their own future museums. For now, Cleveland is preparing a space for its exhibit so today's visitors can enjoy the caprice and wonder of the past.

Where should artifacts go? Is one place better than another, or is each a mere stopover along the well-traveled itinerary of these things? My own preference is that if they cannot remain in situ, they are best curated where they can hold on to as much of their original context as possible. I think back to my friend the bead thief in Arizona, clutching his find and telling me he was now the context for the beads. The trouble was that their new context began and ended with him. He was a blip, a reboot. He found the beads and then lost them. Their story was for him alone, their connection to that cave and to the people who first made or carried them severed.

I believe that the history of artifacts is better served if memory can accompany them. The last known work by Praxiteles would have probably been lost to the dump, so, yes, it is preferable that the Cleveland museum picked up the 2,000-year-old sculpture and reestablished its connection with the past. But reestablishing a connection can mean many things, and, as I discovered, they are not always easy to swallow.

. . .

I was traveling through northern Mexico, stopping frequently to ask if anyone knew about local archaeology. There would always be at least one story about an old farmer who plowed graves out of his field (skeletons, turquoise, shell pendants). On occasion a person would be kind enough to scribble a map onto a rip of paper showing how to find some mound or ruin. In a logging town along the eastern flank of the Sierra Madre I met a man named Mario. At least I think that was his name; his Spanish was so swift I

barely caught it. When I told him I was interested in archaeology Mario brightened. The next day he took me out into
the barrancas, a rifle slung over his shoulder. We followed
game trails into a canyon and found its rocky walls trussed
with many cliff dwellings.

No money was exchanged for his service. Mario simply
wanted me to see what he had also seen, an ancient wealth
of caves stuffed with adobe rooms: black-timbered ceilings,
floors dusted with broken artifacts, a human skull left slack-
jawed on one floor.

Mario and I sat at the edge of a rock outcrop, and he told
me no one else seemed to care about what is out here; everyone was too busy hunting or logging or driving transport
trucks on the highway. To them these ancient things were
fanciful, like fairy tales, things you looked for as a kid.
When drug runners found these ruins they used them as labs
and shelters, knocking down walls for their work. Ranchers
broke open doorways and corralled their cattle inside. There
were few untouched places left, he said, which is why he had
brought me here. He wanted someone else to participate in
his appreciation.

I was heartened to meet a man who shared my impassioned private study of archaeology, and Mario seemed to
feel the same. He invited me back to his house in town: dirt
street, cinderblock walls, front door a strong plank of wood
leaning a bit askew. Young sons and daughters remained at
a polite distance as he beckoned me in, showing me over to
his wooden eating table as his words quickened. It seemed
important to him that I appreciate his table.

My Spanish was rough, but I thought we understood each
other, and I agreed that it was a fine and sturdy table. I
gripped it with my hand to prove the point. As I shook the
table, dried flowers stuck in a gaudy, gold-colored jar rattled at its far end. Probably they were placed there by his

wife, Asucena, who was coming out to greet us, wiping hands dry on her towel.

"O, Asucena, me gusta!" I announced to her, ridiculously.

Mario directed my attention back to the table, slowing his voice as he said, "La olla."

The jar. I turned and realized the jar at the end of the table was pre-Columbian. The room changed shape at that moment. What was this doing here? By its form I could see it was a simple utility vessel that would once have been used for cooking or holding water, a classic of fifteenth-century northern Mexico. Only the color was wrong—it should have been dirt brown, not gold.

"Oro, por qué?" slipped from my mouth. Why gold?

Mario proudly explained that his wife thought the original color was ugly, so he had spray-painted it for her.

My face went blank as I thought, You spray-painted a pre-Columbian jar because your wife didn't like the color?

He waited excitedly for my response. Did I not see it was beautiful, and how well he had chosen? I laughed, but in a pained way, not sure what expression to put on my face. I had thought Mario and I were of like mind, seekers of untouched places. They were, after all, what had drawn Mario and me out there to begin with. Now I was looking at a man who was not only a thief, but a vandal with a can of spray paint. What could I possibly say? It was his house, not a place where a stranger should show alarm. Nor did I have the kind of Spanish at my disposal to say What the hell were you thinking? This thing is an artifact of a lost civilization, and you spray-painted it gold!

"Donde?" I asked.

Mario happily told me he had found it in one of the ruins. I asked if he had dug for it. A little, he said. A touch of shame in his smile said that it had been more than a little.

He explained that there had been another one, much larger and richly painted, but while bringing it out he had lost his grip, dropped it, and now nothing remained but pieces. He described the broken one as a fine specimen of what was probably a Ramos Polychrome, a style he could have easily sold to a passing dealer. I tried not to look sickened as he explained how the second one would have been a nice jar to have in the house, how his wife would have liked all the pretty colors, but it was in so many pieces he could not possibly put it back together. Now it was trash. He was trying to impress me, and I was racking my brain to understand how I had not seen this coming. He was a looter. His wife was a partner in crime, their sweet children accomplices.

Mario asked how old I thought this jar on their table was. His wife watched my lips.

I told them, *"Siete cien años, mas o menos"*—about seven hundred years.

I told you so, he said to her.

She nodded with a small, proud smile and said, *"Es verdad, muy vieja."*

Then I began to notice how the entire family was facing the jar with an almost dignified worshipfulness. They were not looking at the picture of Jesus on the wall, not the fine white propane stove or the couch with a horse blanket over it, but at the jar. It was a beautiful and powerful thing he had brought home. Mario gestured for me to look closely, saying I should notice fingerprints in the clay. The spray paint highlighted them, showing where a potter had once pressed her thumbs into wet clay as she turned back the jar's lip.

"Sí, sí, bonita," Mario said, big smile on his face.

Yes, I had to agree, it was beautiful. Suddenly I felt unsure of what to think about Mario. We were both meddlers snooping along trails of the past, and there was only a slight difference in what we chose to do with what we found. Born to a different family, he might have been an archaeologist or a museum conservator. And born to a different family, I would happily have been a pothunter. I hesitated to speak for fear that I might commit myself, unsure whether I should condemn the man or embrace him for bringing this jar out of the ground and putting it back into use. In a kind of connection with the past I had never even imagined, the jar, and its purpose, were still alive in his home, back on the kitchen table after so many years.

. . .

What would excavators think centuries from now, digging into an early-twenty-first-century Mexican logging village and finding this fifteenth-century jar? Outlier, off the charts, it would be labeled a ritual artifact. Through chemical analysis they would discover traces of gold aerosol paint applied late in its use. Perhaps they would return to their glowing cubes or whatever huts they occupy in the future and marvel at the cyclic wonders of time, how even people of long ago took possession of the past. We find that kind of evidence even now. For instance, a thumb-sized piece of Roman sculpture nearly 2,000 years old was excavated from a native grave in Mexico from the year 1510. However it got there—whether carried across by Columbus's first colonists and traded into indigenous networks or, more unlikely, arrived from Rome on a ship blown terribly off course much earlier—it is a sign of preoccupation with what is old and exotic. We move these things around like charms, and the more of the past they contain, the more powerful they become for us.

All Mario needed to know was that this vessel was old. He did not need to hear the detailed archaeological history of the Casas Grandes culture that occupied the area at the time.

I could understand why Mario had taken the jar, and even why he had painted it. Unburdened by the wider issues of antiquities, he was simply picking up something he found on the ground, even if he had to dig some. With it, he was engaging in his own conversation with history, bringing into his home a human chronicle that reaches back far beyond his own recollection.

Patty Crown, an archaeologist at the University of New Mexico, once told me that objects carried forward could be considered a form of collective memory. Crown was looking at the issue from a scientific perspective, and she was not talking about the likes of Mario. She was studying a cache of artifacts from Chaco Canyon, a thousand-year-old pilgrimage center in the desert of northwest New Mexico. Among a collection of ceremonial jars found there, she recognized signs that they had been repainted and refired numerous times. The tall, narrow jars had originally been painted with painstakingly symmetrical designs that were later whitewashed with a new slip and replaced with another set of painted designs. The vessels were fired once more to seal the new images in place. In some cases this happened more than once, the object retaining its original form while its surface took on a new scheme. In refiring, the kiln temperature had to be the same each time or the vessel would crackle or break.

"Why wouldn't you just throw it away and make a new one?" she asked. "There must have been something important about the object itself." She called keeping a vessel in circulation like this a process of renewal, a way of connecting the past to the present through a physical artifact. It is not just a matter of having the artifact, but changing it.

Often archaeologists use the term *ceremonial* to describe

objects that are difficult to categorize. Even before Crown discovered the subtle histories of these jars, they were being called ceremonial. Only 198 of their kind have been found in the Southwest—tall and slender as wine bottles with the tops cut off, cylinder shaped with flat, open mouths. They were mostly found together in the same ruin and in the same room, and Crown would later discover that they had contained chocolate, thought to be used in rituals. Maybe their repainting was stimulated by something as simple as Mario's wife not liking the color. The original paintings on these important jars might have gone out of style, like 1970s avocado green kitchen appliances. Maybe there were elders who were horrified to see the repaintings and railed that the past was not to be altered. It seems there is a tug-of-war between not touching the past and putting our signature all over it.

I went to New York to see some of the cylinder jars Crown had studied, down in the vaults of the American Museum of Natural History, where they were kept in storage. They lay in deep wooden drawers, and when I lifted them out I could barely see what Crown had deciphered. Beneath their surfaces were the faint lines of ghost paintings. I noticed on each of these vessels small catalogue numbers that had been written in black ink. The perfect, tiny penmanship struck me as yet another layer, a way of ushering these jars into the next era. Now they belong to science.

At some point we draw the line and decree that such actions are vandalism, but I found I could not come to that judgment with Mario. He was not a vandal. Sitting on the table with flowers in it, the jar seemed to me to be back in circulation. This is what this ancient utility vessel was made for to begin with: a good kitchen, a man and a wife, healthy children.

. . .

At the table Mario and I drank Nescafé, and when we were
done I set down the thin white porcelain cup and excused
myself, saying I had many miles to go. I thanked him for all
that he had shown me.

Knowing that we would never see each other again,
Mario and I did not share addresses. Friendships are brief
on the road. At the door Mario said he had a gift, in gratitude for my visit. He held out a stone axe head, a rough
piece of rounded basalt. He had dug it up near the jar. A
notch ran down its middle where the wooden handle would
have been attached. With my interest in archaeology, he figured this was a good choice.

I declined as politely as I could, saying it was too *muy
excelente* a gift. He kept pushing it toward me until I felt my
refusal might be taken as rude. I finally accepted it, and was
surprised by its weight—it was heavy as a brick. I gave
Mario a small, grateful bow, praising him, his wife, and
their beaming children as I backed out the front door with
the gift in my hand.

The axe head was not mine, though. I did not want the
commitment it represented; I did not want to escort it
through time. My mind ran circles of logic around it as it sat
on the floorboards of my truck. I thought of pulling over
and leaving it on the roadside, returning it to the general
country it came from, a quick thank-you and good-bye. But
it was an honest gift from a family with few but precious
belongings, one not to be treated lightly. What could I make
of it? A doorstop maybe, a paperweight, an offering on a
makeshift altar?

I felt I was now at the very root of the antiquities continuum, the bottom of the ownership scale, a range that starts

with an axe head (or a spray-painted jar) and ends with eight-digit purchases of Greek artifacts carefully touched up for auction. It is all about moving pieces of the past into their new locations, their next in situ.

When I reached the border I rolled down my window and a man with mirrored eyes looked in. He asked if I had any illicit things in my vehicle—artifacts, specimens, contraband. I looked back at him and said no.

~~~~~~~~~~~

CHAPTER 11

HOUSES OF OBSESSION

There was an old man named John Eaton who could not stop collecting. His house was a ramshackle array of coins and knives and nearly everything else he had ever found or bought or dug out of the ground himself. He was a self-proclaimed pothunter who said he had grown up doing it because he loved having things around that took him back in time. In his eighties, he almost giddily showed me from room to room, through piles and stacks, opening cabinets, pulling out drawers. He wore a starched white shirt buttoned at his wrists, his skin a powdery white, as if he were preparing himself for a coffin. With jittery hands he pressed objects into mine, arrow shafts, Confederate bills, a Navajo squash blossom of silver and turquoise. You could hardly move through the house and its claptrap miscellany. Sometimes you can understand why archaeologists might see people like this as an abomination, bereft of scientific values. All they do is collect.

If you read the voluminous academic literature covering archaeological ethics, you will notice an almost unanimous chant of *private-collectors-are-bad*. If you happen to read the much smaller body of literature put out by the collectors themselves—including letters to the editor and the volatile ramblings of numismatists—you might tend to agree with the assessment. Collectors can be a bit odd, mentally sideways and occasionally brilliant. At the same time, every one I have met has offered a spark of inspiration. They have their own window into the past.

Mr. Eaton had invited me over to show off the pre-Columbian portion of his artifact collection. Some things, he told me, he had gotten with a shovel, and some he had purchased. But he could not seem to remember where they were. In his living room, which looked like a collision between Pier One and an antiques rummage sale, he was resting on a couch, while I sat in a chair across from him. Nothing in the room was more than a century and a half old. He seemed to have forgotten why he had invited me over. Senility appeared to overtake him, his memory draining away almost by the minute. I asked again about the artifacts.

"They're here, aren't they?" he asked, looking around in confusion.

His son, fifty years old and beginning to gray a bit himself, sat down on a nearby couch and said, "Dad...Dad... you sold the last baskets a couple months ago."

"Sold?" Mr. Eaton asked, surprised. "Oh, yes. What was it?"

"Somebody called, you remember? An art collector. He came down and paid two thousand dollars each."

Mr. Eaton gave a small sound of recognition.

The son, who is personally opposed to pothunting, having left behind a pot he and his son once found in the desert, looked at me. "Is that a good price, two thousand?"

"What kind of baskets were they?" I inquired.

Mr. Eaton began describing them, his lifted hands forming baskets bigger than his head, coil weave by the sound of it. Although much of his mind had been lost, he maintained an astonishing memory for certain details. It struck me that his artifacts will probably be the last thing he recalls. When names and faces finally fail him, he will still see the spiral coil of a woven basket that he once lifted out of the ground with his own hands, uncapping someone's burial.

The style of basket sounded as if it had come from a couple of thousand years ago, made by people who buried their dead with baskets on top of them. Some of the finest weavers in North America, they were a well-looted bunch. I told the son, "You could have gotten more."

He said, "I didn't want him to sell them. It's hard when I don't live here."

Mr. Eaton was still looking perplexed. "Are you sure they're not in the house somewhere?"

The son shook his head. "They're gone."

His father's collection had been steadily leaking away over the years. Sold? Given away? Lost? No telling where the pieces all ended up. The son explained to me that his father would die soon and all this would be his. "I know so few of these stories," he said. "I don't know how I'm going to do this."

Mr. Eaton levered himself up from the couch and managed to find his ledger, a book press-labeled "The Silent Secretary," circa 1960. He handed it to me open to his own illustrations of artifacts he had found, roughly copied designs from ceramic vessels, the flourish of early Pueblo pottery. I thumbed through pages of jars, bowls, axe heads, projectile points. A scribble of notes accompanied each illustration but no mention of context, location, anything that would tie the artifact back to a place. He was an archaeologist at heart, not just a voracious, hard-assed consumer of antiquities but a methodical searcher with almost scientific inclinations, but he had no training.

Mr. Eaton explained that he had been collecting since he was a kid growing up in the Four Corners. All his life he was drawn to antiquity, and people would even bring their possessions to him as if he were a repository, a safer place than their own homes.

He reminisced, "They were everywhere. You hardly had to dig. You'd just see a pot sticking out of the ground. Of course I took them. Who wouldn't? They were treasures."

The last of his treasures were now drifting through the antiquities market in a much larger world, joining the goods of Africa, Europe, and Asia, and leaving him alone with his ledger.

This is what happens to collections. They eventually fly apart. They are held as long as possible, but the owner's grip loosens. It is a principal dilemma of archaeology. Objects so much older than ourselves are bound to outlive our fascinations. Author Ernest Becker, in his book *Denial of Death,* proposed the notion of "immortality projects." According to Becker, these projects are what we create to outlast what he sees as the meaninglessness of our own deaths. Politics, philosophies, institutions, statues, anything we can pull together that will live longer than we do, are a bid for a kind of immortality. Artifact collections perfectly fit the bill. They are a way of reaching far beyond our era, into both the past and the future.

Sitting with Mr. Eaton felt more like a mortality project than an immortality one. Nothing says "your fragile life will blink out" like an old man who cannot remember what happened to all the ancient things he collected. When I said good-bye to him at his front door, we shook hands and I felt the bones of his fingers, his soft, cool skin thin as vellum.

. . .

Imagine having your own private collection of artifacts, museum-quality stock. You are the sole authority decreeing who can see them and who cannot. They are yours to admire

at your leisure, a slice of history at your fingertips, an obsession all your own.

While this may be a fantasy for many, it is a reality for a
select number of collectors around the world. Art Cooper is
one. A retired physician, he has turned his ranch-style home
into an artifact repository for pre-Columbian ceramics.

"I have visited many of the great archaeological sites
in the world," he told me when I visited him. "To own something of a past civilization is to better understand it and put
the present in perspective. To live with something from that
civilization is to have a spiritual connection with it."

Neighbors were unaware of the wealth of antiquities
stored in this house. Besides some Mayan ceramics and a
handful of early-Pueblo pots from the Four Corners, the
bulk of the collection consisted of colorful northern Mexican wares from around the fifteenth century.

We were in the living room, the space around us loaded
with pots—walls, shelves, tables—categorically arranged
into monochromes, polychromes, effigies. As he plucked
down the finer ones to show me, his wife, Betty, stood back
watching with a pleasant air of circumspection. It was not
often they let a stranger into their home. I don't blame them;
they had nearly three hundred vessels in their house, the
highest-valued piece worth $50,000, probably half a million
dollars in total for the collection. They guarded it assiduously, with deadbolts and a commercial security system.

Some of their vessels came from an art museum that was
selling overstock but most were purchased from dealers.
Some came directly from a man in cowboy boots who lived
in southern New Mexico (guaranteeing that they were
unearthed on private land). Although they swore he was not
a pothunter, he certainly fit the description.

A large man but not fat, hands clasped before him, Art said
they used to lend their best pieces to museums for exhibitions,

but it no longer feels safe to do so. Private collectors they know have gotten nailed as soon as they put their pieces on display. Questions pop up, federal agents come knocking at their doors.

Not surprisingly, Art does not like how things have turned out, with private collectors now the pariahs of the archaeological community.

"Few are allowed to touch or even cherish these ancient objects," Art argued. My head nodded involuntarily.

"There have been collectors from time immemorial," he said. "Archaeologists are but johnny-come-latelies with an attitude that only they have a right to collect and interpret the past."

I nodded at that, too. But knowing that this is not a clean business, I could not help having reservations. Private collectors are on their own: they have no rules, no agreed-upon principles. Most operate below the radar, their artifact sources shady. Many enter the market without any awareness of what may have been destroyed to bring them their treasure. Trace any of these objects back through time and there will always be a boot and a shovel — and likely there is scant or no scientifically useful provenance.

The principal argument against private collection is clear. For every object on the shelf there is a hole in a grave, an emptied tomb, a ransacked archaeological site with no record to be followed. In June 2008, 929 pre-Columbian artifacts, not unlike the ones the Coopers own, were returned to Mexico after being seized by customs agents in Texas, Arizona, and Toronto. They had been smuggled out of the country. This is a small sample of the more than nineteen thousand objects that Mexico's National Anthropology Institute says have been sent back to Mexico from the United States and Canada over a five-year period.

I have traveled in the source region of most of the ceramics the Coopers hold. It's why I had come to their house. I wanted to see where the pots had gone. All along the flanks of the Sierra Madre Occidental the looting damage is difficult to miss. I found one canyon full of big adobe cliff dwellings that looked as if someone had taken a sledgehammer to them. I dubbed the place Rape Canyon. Doorways were busted open, elevated granaries were cut down one after the next, their contents spilled as if they were piñatas. Only top-shelf material had been taken, the looters leaving junk heaps of decayed textiles and bone-dry corncobs. To get to their precious polychromes, they had disfigured other remains in the way, putting their shovels straight through skeletons and plain-ware ollas, laying waste to history.

When I asked Art how he felt about this end of the problem, he said he buys only objects that have been on the market for so long that it hardly matters. His collection was the end result of long-past transgressions, the looters' pits already healed over.

The tide of professional opinion, however, is against him. Museums are urged not to display private collections unless their provenance is unassailable. Scholars are being pressured to avoid any study of them. If an artifact gets a nod from a PhD, its price shoots up. The American Institute of Archaeology refuses even to publish or review work that involves undocumented artifacts like many in the Coopers' collection. (You may be able to determine by inscriptions on a vessel that it came from Paquimé in Chihuahua in the fifteenth century, but if there is no literal account, no record of the grave or room it came from, it is rejected.) To modern science, what the Coopers have is virtually worthless, but to the Coopers, it is a source of another kind of knowledge, a personal way of comprehending the past. In the years they have spent studying their vessels, they have gained a deep familiarity with them, which they feel has given them insight into interpreting the meaning behind many of their design elements.

Art picked up a bold pre-Columbian effigy jar the size of a coffee mug. He said he had bought it on eBay a few days earlier, a startlingly fine example of Ramos Polychrome, especially for an Internet buy. It was a richly painted Neolithic figurine, a woman with fat legs and skinny arms in a seated position, her vagina a slice in the clay surrounded by the rise of her vulva. Judging by the style, she probably came from within at least a couple of hundred miles of the raped landscape I had seen.

"We paid two thousand dollars online," Art said, chuckling. "It's actually worth more around ten thousand."

The Internet has lately become a key resource for buyers, and although many scholars feared this would drive the market through the roof, according to Charles Stanish of the Department of Anthropology at UCLA, it has had the opposite effect. Sellers have started making more fakes, which has had a surprisingly chilling effect on the looting industry. Stanish noticed the change around 2000. He said that "the local eBayers and craftsmen can make more money cranking out cheap fakes than they can by spending days or weeks digging around looking for the real thing." The reward for illicit digging, he noted, decreases every time someone buys a "genuine" pre-Columbian pot for $35 plus shipping and handling.

Forgeries are becoming so good that even experts are having trouble weeding them out. One forger in Italy was caught exposing his vessels to radiation at a cancer treatment ward so they would pass the thermoluminescence tests that determine age (they even slipped past experts at the British Museum). And there was the 2002 uproar over the "James Ossuary," a stone that supposedly proved the existence of Jesus's brother. After receiving high marks from key scholars, it turned out to be an ancient blank tablet that was later inscribed, the letters carefully brushed with patina so they would blend in. The deception ruined entire careers.

Despite all this, Art swore he was not being duped. "My eye has gotten better at spotting forgeries," he insisted. "This one is the real thing. There's just something you can detect in a fake, something wrong with it. I've gotten to where I can spot one from across the room."

Art drew out a book of artifacts from a museum in Mexico. He opened it to a page displaying a photo of the very effigy jar I held in my hands.

"See?" he said. "It's real."

Looking at a museum artifact identical to this one, I was not sure how to respond. Had it been stolen? Confused, I glanced at Art, hoping he had a good answer for me.

"Look more closely," he said.

I did. The vessel in the book looked identical, until I realized the two were actually opposites of each other, like bookends.

"Is the photo reversed?" I asked.

"No," Art said. "They're different. Look at these lines here, and here. They don't match up. These were made as a pair, twins."

I puzzled for a moment, wondering if fakes have become this good. I said, "From the same grave, you think?"

Art smiled as if I were finally reading his mind. "Exactly. That's what I've thought, too."

"Then how were they separated?"

"Who knows? Maybe they were excavated at two different times."

I said, "The museum would know where it came from."

Art nodded silently.

"You're sure it's not a fake, a replica of the original?" I asked.

"Who would reproduce an exact opposite?"

Later, Art would ask me not to mention the name of the museum to anyone. He laughingly added that he and Betty preferred to keep out of the limelight.

Holding the round clay woman in my hands, I asked, "Would you ever turn this over, so the two could be paired up?"

Art looked at me, startled.

. . .

One of the world's great collectors, George Ortiz, describes how and why he is affected by antiquities: "The vision of certain objects struck me viscerally, then they came to fascinate and move me, I let them speak to me, I let their content and spirit nourish me." In this sense, the love for artifacts is about the object itself and what it emotionally conveys. This is what rankles many scholars and archaeologists, that the object is seen as *art,* with no real need for detailed social, cultural, or geographic context. Collectors go more by feel. What they feel is historicity.

Historicity means historical authenticity. It is a quality that objects possess, the difference between last night's bottle cap and a medallion carried around the neck of a conquistador. When a thing has seen centuries, it builds up historicity. When a copy of the Magna Carta sold at auction for $21.3 million, it was not the paper itself or the hand-lettered words on it that fetched such a price, but the sense of what it was. The concept is best explained in Philip K. Dick's *The Man in the High Castle.*

She said, "What is 'historicity'?"

"When a thing has history in it. Listen. One of those two Zippo lighters was in Franklin D. Roosevelt's pocket when he was assassinated. And one wasn't. One has historicity, a hell of a lot of it. As much as any object ever had. And one has nothing."

The Coopers' house was filled with historicity. Hundreds of vessels led up and out of a sunken living room into big display cases standing against the walls. There were even pots in the kitchen; the Coopers' refrigerator was topped by a row of painted jars, all bird effigies, likenesses of macaws and parrots that reminded me of the tawdry chickens and roosters you often see in American kitchens.

I asked him what he would eventually do with it all. Art turned to me and pleaded, "This collection has to be taken as a whole, a sum of its parts. I don't want it piecemealed."

One has to wonder what was piecemealed to get these artifacts together in the first place. How many grave assemblages were scattered for his archaeological rhapsody? The plan, Art said, was to bequeath the collection to their heirs in the hope they would keep it together. Yet this collection will probably be scattered again to feed other collections, just as John Eaton's was.

I asked Art if they had considered bequeathing the collection to a museum, which might keep it intact longer. Art said he would not let that happen. He fears that certain vessels might be confiscated in federal raids targeting unsavory dealers. He wants them together, here, telling a story he reads each time he passes through his house.

. . .

I found myself simultaneously accepting of and disgusted by the Coopers. There are arguments that favor them, such as the idea that material history is not the sole possession of institutions. Everyday citizens should not be barred from such a direct connection with the past. Souren Melikian, an erudite arts correspondent, wrote in the *New York Times*,

"Private connoisseurship is the crucial element that paradoxically guarantees the freedom of looking at art other than by institutional decree, in an environment, lighting and presentation included, that is not predetermined."

Arguments against the Coopers tend to be more far-reaching. Their lust for artifacts results in unrecorded sites being permanently destroyed in order to feed a greed-driven and object-based market. Beyond the damage on the ground, most professional conservators would find the idea of keeping pre-Columbian pots in a kitchen—exposing them to heat, steam, and grease—tantamount to vandalism. Unlike elite professional repositories, the Coopers' house is not kept at an even 55°F, nor is there a hydrometer registering steady 70 percent humidity.

I felt an impulse to alert the museum in Mexico to the missing twin effigy jar, or at least to mention to authorities the name of a dealer possibly working as a pothunter in New Mexico. But that would have been a violation of the Coopers' hospitality. They wanted me to see what they had gathered and their efforts at preservation. That, I respected. Confiscating their collection and transferring it to the black hole of a lockdown facility seemed ludicrous.

For this moment the vessels belong to the Coopers. This is their context, the place they are most deeply appreciated. This house is now a finely decorated tomb, a wealth of carefully chosen history that Art and Betty have gathered around themselves. I felt grateful that they had let me in and that they were so free with their enthusiasm. Indeed, they wholeheartedly believed they were doing the right thing.

Art urged me to touch anything that caught my eye, beckoning me to hold vessels in my hands and examine them for however long I wished. He wanted me to fully appreciate them. Even among museum curators I had never seen such passion: each object was tenderly cradled in Art's hands as he passed it to me and then took it back.

The question of whether private collections should be allowed is almost irrelevant. While they are often crimes of degrees, a matter of steps from ransacked archaeological sites, they are not going away. Ancient things have always moved from hand to hand. They do not belong to a black-and-white ethic, rather they are part of the myriad relationships that arise from our fascination with the past and its objects. These artifacts do not merely serve our wide-ranging purposes. They manipulate us as well.

We retired to the porch for tea. In the sunshine Betty laughed and admitted that they had no idea such issues existed when they had begun collecting in the 1990s. They hadn't suspected so many scholars were opposed to private collection. She eyed me and said, "I am curious what you think."

"I think it's a mess," I said. "Once you touch it, once it's out of the ground, there's no one right thing to do. I don't think anyone can honestly take the moral high ground."

Betty smiled and said, "Exactly."

I said, "One way or another I think we are all thieves."

Art bristled at that. He said, "That's not quite what we mean. We consider ourselves more temporary custodians."

"Yes," I conceded. "Of course."

I figured every whole pot in their collection had come from a grave. Does it matter how long ago? The ground is being emptied so that these things can be possessed. This isn't just about stewardship. It is an obsession that runs the gamut of our desires.

~~~~~~~~~~

CHAPTER 12

PUBLIC TRUST

I have relished museums. There is a silence they offer, a hush that saturates the air. Even museums where mothers shout for their children, where waves of toddlers rush chattering through exhibits, even they have private, interior vaults that shut out every sound but your own footsteps. Some museums sound like vast air ducts, some like the inside of tombs still sealed. There are darkened spaces where lights flicker on as you enter a storage room filled chockablock with artifacts, and those lit like chemistry labs, not a shadow lurking among perfect rows of vessels.

However artifacts found their way to museums, by whatever subterfuge or illusion, they offer an experience close to what I have gotten in the wilderness, ducking behind a boulder to find a hidden jar. In a museum you roam from hall to hall, drifting through the past in whatever form suits you, whether you see the hands of ancients or the chiseling work of archaeologists and looters. Rather than languishing in the half light of private collections, artifacts in museums are a common wealth. Institutional storage rooms are available to anyone with the credentials to gain access and crack open the next mystery. When Patty Crown discovered chocolate residues inside pre-Columbian vessels from New Mexico, it was the first evidence of chocolate ever found in North America, a major leap in understanding the relationship between the Southwest and Mesoamerica. She found this not by digging fresh specimens but through years of searching the back rooms of museums, sorting through thousands of vessels and sherds. There are discoveries to be made in these halls.

Museums contain so many objects that what a visitor sees on display is, on average, a mere half a percent of the institution's holdings. The remainder is sequestered not because of greed, but by necessity. Exhibiting everything would be chaos, with the beauty of individual artifacts eclipsed by sheer volume. Even Thomas Hoving thought some of the Met's halls were overloaded, contending that only the best items should be shown. Everything else should go into storage that's restricted to scholars, he said, safe from the uninformed masses who cannot tell Euphronios from Lydos.

Given a choice, if artifacts could not safely rest in the ground, I would have them in museums. There are so many; encyclopedic museums like the Met, where one returns again and again and always finds something new, or the well-stocked regional museums such as Edge of the Cedars in Blanding, Utah, the most comprehensive displays of Anasazi peoples. If I had to choose one institution for its overall tenor, the place I have most appreciated, it would be the Peabody Museum of Archaeology and Ethnology in Cambridge, Massachusetts, whose public spaces are weighted with an irresistible stillness. Since 1868 the Peabody, one of the oldest museums in the world devoted solely to human antiquity, has occupied an expansive Victorian manor on the Harvard University campus. There are no stuffed rabbits, triceratops parts, or pressed plants—only human artifacts, six million of them when you count the collection at the bead-and-sherd level.

Sliding my hand down a wooden banister, I followed

Susan Haskell, one of the Peabody's many curators and technicians, to the first floor, striding across its polished surface with our white lab coats swishing around our legs. Haskell held a key ring as big as a manacle from which hung keys of many shapes and sizes — keys for deadbolts and padlocks, keys to open drawers, keys for safety boxes. She jangled one out, unlocked a door, and told me to watch my step. A wooden staircase descended through groaning furnace pipes. At the bottom another key opened another door, and Haskell ushered me into the dust-free North American Ethnographic Collections Area. The space sounded like the slow draw of large bellows. Its prime function being environmental control, its air was kept circulating, and its temperature and humidity were maintained as if everything were held in suspended animation.

I had come to spend a few days studying the remains of Awat'ovi, a legendary pueblo that stands on the dry and brindled mesas of northeast Arizona. A four-thousand-room settlement belonging to the ancestors of the modern Hopi, the pueblo has been reduced to windswept mounds where you can hardly walk without crackling across broken pottery. In the mid-1930s the Peabody did thorough work at Awat'ovi, excavating, mapping, collecting, and shifting artifacts to Harvard, some two thousand miles away.

We began with murals that had been peeled out of the ceremonial kivas. Haskell turned a corner to a wall hung with these fragmented paintings, stepping aside as if tipping open a curtain for me. Originally, the underground kivas of Awat'ovi had been elaborately painted from floor to ceiling with multicolored murals of rituals and life-size scenes from ancient stories. To excise the murals, Peabody workers excavated the kivas, cleaned the walls, and coated them with resin, which they then covered with burlap. When the resin dried, they pulled off the burlap and the murals came free.

We slowly moved from one to the next, studying their forms. Had they been top priority for conservation, they would have been laid flat in drawers and covered, but as one conservator told me, museum work is like triage: managers looking at limited budgets have to decide what is of prime concern, what is most fragile. The murals are doing fine on the walls. In fact, I was glad to see them positioned vertically, much the way they were when excavated. In an echo of ancient practice, they are hidden from public display in an underground space where people can come only by special permission. This is not so different from the tradition of kivas themselves.

I stepped close to a nearly-life-size woman rendered in sixteenth-century geometric form. She was detailed down to her pulled-back hair and the colorful weave of her dress. Her face looked like a mask.

The modern Hopi would never allow me into a place like this. Theirs is a culture rigid with tradition and orthodoxy, and ritual images are reserved for certain clans or societies. Many Hopi I've spoken with are simply bewildered at the way their ancestors and so many of their trappings are being dug up. It seems grotesque. Before coming here I had asked a tribal archaeologist if he thought there might be a problem with my seeing the murals. He laughed and said it would be different if I were Hopi and I had any idea what I was looking at. No, I could stare as I wished.

I moved closer to the masked woman and looked into the sly cuts of her eyes, all the while thinking she belonged to a clan or to a sacred society, part of the ritual fabric of people long dead.

"I hadn't realized they were so detailed," I said.

Haskell nodded.

Another figure with a mask held a long-tailed bird in his right hand and what looked like a tropical macaw perched on his shoulder. Brilliantly stylized, they looked like early Hopi art deco.

Most painted kivas found in the Southwest have been destroyed by weather or vandals, and these are some of the few murals found intact. Their good condition is owed partly to the Spanish, who in the seventeenth century used the kivas as a foundation for a Franciscan mission. It is owed also to the native laborers who filled the kivas with clean sand before the mission was built, packing the murals neatly away as if for a long journey.

Another reason for the degree of preservation, besides the fact that they have been kept in a museum for the past several decades, is that Awat'ovi itself was eventually destroyed and left uninhabited. After construction of the mission, the pueblo fell to a sneak attack by an alliance of three rival pueblos, on a night when Spanish and native Awat'ovi residents alike were killed. Rarely do Hopi wage war, but when they do, it is thorough, designed to wipe a place and its people off the map. In this case, men of Awat'ovi were burned alive in the remaining kivas, and those trying to climb ladders and escape out ceiling hatches were shot with arrows. Women were marched away, many killed, some beheaded. Like a taboo, Awat'ovi was left untouched, its history allowed to sink into oblivion until the Peabody expedition arrived with shovels, trowels, burlap, and trucks. This is what artifacts in museums often mean. They are cut from places often left intentionally vacant: graves, tombs, and shrines. The intrusion gets blotted out by perfect lighting.

Haskell stood behind me, hands clasped at her back.

Looking closely at the paintings I said, "It's probably best they aren't on public display. I mean, the way the Hopi are with private matters."

I felt torn in two, half of me relishing what the museum

had collected, the other half back on the edge of a mesa, aware of a troubling vacuum underfoot. Though resin and burlap were state of the art in 1936, the technique is fundamentally destructive, allowing only one layer of paintings to survive. Often kiva murals were made a hundred layers thick, with one on top of the last. Excavators at Awat'ovi assiduously flaked off paint to reach the one mural they could best salvage. How many others were permanently destroyed in the process?

"We would never do this today, of course," Haskell said. "There are many different nondestructive techniques that could be used now."

Like many curators I have met, Haskell seemed preternaturally attentive, as if standing on the tips of her toes with a pen, ready to scribble a catalogue number across my forehead and slap me in a drawer. Her presence at my side every time I moved down the hall was a constant reminder of how carefully these artifacts have been curated.

Haskell led me around a corner, where we found a segment of a Hopi mural propped on a shelf. Facing it, in shocking contrast, was an artful raven from the Northwest coast. She made a surprised sound when she saw the two. The raven was dark and brazenly animist; the Hopi work seemed flowery, otherworldly.

She hurriedly picked up the flat piece of Hopi mural and carried it to a nearby table, where she rested it faceup.

"I'm sorry," she said to me. "Things need to be kept in better order. Those two shouldn't be together."

She paced quickly down an aisle to a woman, a museum technician, who was sitting at a table writing labels.

"Who's been working in the murals?" Haskell demanded.

The technician looked up, eyes focusing on Haskell. An apologetic response followed.

Returning, Haskell explained the museum has strict protocols and having two different cultures together like that, even in storage, is not allowed. "We keep Pueblo artifacts with Pueblo artifacts, Northwest with Northwest," she said.

At this level of curation, discriminations are even subtler than that. Depending on requests from various cultural groups, artifacts may be treated on an individual basis. Some are kept covered, some are positioned to face a particular cardinal direction, and some are kept out of view of women. Here in the underworld of a museum, science and the sacred meet. Hopi representatives have come to the Peabody on occasion and left offerings of fresh tobacco and cornmeal that the museum carefully monitors. Technicians place the offerings in plastic containers to prevent contamination but make sure to leave holes in the tops to allow the offerings to interact with the artifacts in what might be called a spiritual manner.

If there is any way to properly curate plunder—including objects removed by bona fide archaeologists decades ago— it seems to be this. The museum has become a kind of church, a kiva, where Haskell and I moved in our long white coats like abbots of another age.

· · ·

Not all public collections are this fortunate. In 2004, looking for certain specimens, I visited Wendy Bustard at the Chaco Museum Collection in Albuquerque. She and I pulled open cardboard boxes and felt down through plastic sacks in a basement with shelves and boxes stacked sixteen feet high, under white ceiling tiles piss-stained from broken plumbing upstairs. Bustard was not simply embarrassed by the condition of her collection, she was mad. She wanted something far better and was not getting it, her budget falling short of what was needed to keep the repository at even a marginal level.

At the time of my visit, Bustard had little financial support as she oversaw one million artifacts stored in six different federal repositories. She had pointed at the notebook in my hands and said, "Write it down. Somebody needs to hear that our collections are not doing well. I don't even have the funding to hire a curator."

But things soon turned around for her. As a National Park Service institution, Bustard's collection was unexpectedly granted federal funding shortly after my visit, enough for entirely new storage and research laboratories situated on the University of New Mexico campus, a success story complete with a new curator.

But good news is thin these days. One conservator told me, "No one in the museum world has enough money, not even the Smithsonian. People are struggling to get $150,000 grants, and still it covers nothing."

A recent study of objects held in public trust in the United States found that of 4.8 billion items, including 44 million feet of archival records (more than 8,300 miles of manuscripts and maps), 820 million specimens are in need of help—some urgently. Meanwhile, 1.8 billion artifacts remain in unknown condition, many unchecked since the day they were put in storage. The study concluded that action is needed to prevent the imminent destruction of up to 190 million objects. Redundant soil samples are being thrown out, while stocks of ancient coins, pots, and statuary are taken from storage and liquidated for cash in a procedure known as deaccessioning. (According to national museum standards, proceeds from deaccessions can be used only to better the existing collection.) Even the Peabody at Harvard has felt the pinch, which is a very bad sign for all the museums down the line. Money tends to go to other projects first.

. . .

After we left the murals, Haskell and I walked across campus in our lab coats, past a lunch truck with faculty standing in line. On the other side of a parking lot stood a metal structure three stories tall, the museum's ceramics storage. As we climbed stairs to its second-story entry, she explained that the adjacent science lab had been pushing to expand, which would require three feet of new foundation space, which in turn meant that the entire ceramics storage facility would have to come down. If the building were to be demolished, artifacts would need to be relocated, at a cost of about $10 million. Relocation did not mean transferring them to a new facility, however, but scattering them to more affordable locations throughout the city, where access would be greatly diminished. This did not happen, though, not this time. The science lab expansion was eventually halted, the ceramics collection allowed to remain. But as funding leaks away from museums, the threat hovers. What has taken thousands of years to accumulate in one place could easily be thrown back to the wind as a country's priorities shift through the decades. Though museums are one of the safest places to keep what has been already gathered, it is not certain that they will endure. A woman overseeing a government-owned collection of historic American artifacts kept in a barn once said to me, "Every time the wind blows through those crevices you just know it's going away."

"Museums just aren't priority," Haskell said as she swiped a magnetic key and the door released. Inside, the first thing we saw was a stone jaguar, a Mayan carving put here because it had nowhere else to go. We slid past and entered a miraculous arena of ceramics. A space the size of a high school gymnasium was packed floor to ceiling with pots on three separate levels. Through the metal-grate floors you could see from one level to the next. As we clanked down a staircase and turned across the floor, I found myself overtaken with a bit of vertigo, staring up and then down at thousands of slender-handled jars, brown-clay effigies, and bowls stacked inside each other (foam cushions nestled between each). The profusion was stunning.

Seeing the look on my face, Haskell said, "I feel the same way every time I come here."

I had never seen so many vessels in my life. It looked like a china factory warehouse, only each of these was a priceless artifact.

We set off looking for pots collected from Awat'ovi. It took a while, since it is nearly impossible for any curator to recall the location of each artifact in a given collection. Part of what took so long, though, was Haskell's evident pleasure as she paused, admiring random and attractive vessels, then slipping on cotton gloves to lift them from their shelves. I was pleased to be with her, taken by her enthusiasm. I have heard private collectors accuse professionals of being heartless overseers of their stockpiles. Haskell was far from that. She thanked me for getting her out of the office, saying that she appreciates every opportunity she gets to enter the collection.

"This one always catches my eye," she said, picking up a white jar the size of a watermelon, its surface bolted with black symmetrical lightning. "It's hard to just walk by it."

I recognized the jar from a report I'd seen, a Peabody paper from the late 1800s.

Excitedly I said, "It's from a site down near the Utah-Arizona border."

Haskell smiled at me, and I felt for the first time that I was of some small use to her.

"It's in this big arc of a canyon," I continued, "a long line of masonry cliff dwellings up in the sandstone, and some big springs, weeping walls full of maidenhair ferns. It's quite a beautiful place."

Setting the jar back on the shelf, she said, "I hadn't known."

These items were too far north for Awat'ovi, and we continued down the aisles, picking through monochrome pots, until we reached a brilliant array of colors, jars as broad and stylized as flying saucers painted in reds, yellows, blacks, and whites. This was Awat'ovi.

As we picked out jars one at a time, rotating them overhead to see the smooth shapes of their bottoms, I felt as if we were breaking into a time capsule. We could see the very brushstrokes of potters who had lived when Awat'ovi was a huge and thriving pueblo, one of the largest in the Southwest. These vessels held the sounds of barking dogs and children running through plazas, the hard grind of stone on corn, and the mumble of old men sitting in wall shade.

Mindful of the threat posed by the nearby science lab, I wondered if this would be the last time these pots would be seen together. It would be a shame, I thought, but perhaps it was an inevitability. More than science labs threaten these collections. Foreign countries are leveraging the return of artifacts like the Euphronios and Aphrodite, while Native Americans, Australian Aborigines, and other indigenous peoples occupying tiny remnant territories around the world are demanding repatriation of their stolen materials, the booty of colonialism and genocide. (After the passage of NAGPRA, the Peabody alone returned the remains of two thousand individuals and more than three thousand artifacts.) The steady collecting of centuries is beginning to recede.

At the same time, major museums around the world are being hit by costly thefts, sometimes perpetrated in broad daylight by armed men in ski masks, and sometimes by unscrupulous curators stealing from the inside. In 2006, $5 million in objects were found to be missing from the Hermitage in St. Petersburg, leakage that turned out to have been partly orchestrated by curator Larisa Zavadskaya. While her collection was being inventoried by authorities to determine what was missing, Zavadskaya died of a heart attack at her desk.

Then there are the cases of utter devastation, such as the once-acclaimed National Museum of Afghanistan near Kabul, which was hit by rockets in 1993. An institution caught on the front lines of a factional war, its vaulted roof caught fire and crashed into the upper galleries. Later, soldiers and other looters sorted through the rubble, removing nearly two-thirds of the museum's holdings, a priceless assortment of artifacts that ranged from Macedonian to Buddhist.

Consider also Iraq and the 2003 looting of the National Library and Archives, where 1.2 million books were destroyed. Next the Central Library of the Ministry of Endowments and Religious Affairs, the oldest cultural institution in the nation, burned to the ground. Most famous was the looting of the National Museum of Iraq, one of the world's largest repositories of Mesopotamian and Sumerian artifacts going back 7,000 years. For three days during the American invasion of Baghdad, hundreds of looters wandered the museum unchecked, shattering glass cases and beating down locked doors. Donny George Youkhanna, an Assyrian archaeologist who was museum director at the time, came back to find his desk in three or four pieces, his chair three hundred feet away, papers scattered two feet deep in his office. He said it looked as if a hurricane had hit from the inside. Prior to the invasion, he had had enough time to evacuate only the most portable top-shelf antiquities to vaults in the Central Bank. After that, more than thirteen thousand artifacts went missing in an anarchic furor, men smashing what they could not take. American forces had been carrying a short list of places to protect, and number two was the National Museum. The Ministry of Oil was number sixteen, near the bottom. Journalists at the time joked that the military must have read the list upside down: while the oil ministry was crawling with American tanks, no one showed up at the museum.

Some of the looters were common thieves who filled sacks as quickly as they could with jewels, vessels, and parts of statues knocked off with baseball bats. Others were far more methodical, showing up with glass cutters and keys. These men knew exactly what they were after: artifacts that would move quickly on the market. They reached the inner rooms by breaking in through a small screened window and from there walked past replicas of artifacts that would have tricked the general public. Youkhanna said he thought smugglers had been carefully preparing for that day, with artifacts perhaps sold even before the invasion started.

In those first days, as Baghdad rang with explosions and gunfire, Youkhanna encountered a breed of looter he had not expected, a group of young men who went into the museum with everyone else, indistinguishable from crazed hoi polloi. They had grabbed nine major pieces, and a few days later approached Youkhanna and one of his curators. They had, they explained, been able to save some of the artifacts. The young men said that the looters had been armed with guns and knives, and there had been no sense opposing them. Instead, they simply blended in and like everyone else hauled off what they could. Once the young men were assured that the nine pieces would be safe, that the museum was again secure, they brought them back bundled in fabric. They weren't the only ones. Soon a man and his brother brought artifacts he had been able to salvage, slipping into the museum along with the rampaging crowds.

For Youkhanna, the return of each artifact was crucial. He told me that archaeology is the substance of history. "Without these documents—whether statue or clay tablet—we would be lacking proof. Each one tells us the story. It tells everything in a pure language."

The Baghdad museum's losses have been trickling back in, over half of what was originally stolen returning within five years. Items have surfaced in raids and stings, and in the suitcases of American attachés passing through customs, trying to get relics home. In 2008, Jordanian border officials alone seized 2,466 figurines, vessels, beads, seals, coins, and scrolls. But most of the key missing pieces have gone underground and will not appear again for a generation or two. Some will vanish entirely to the caprices of war and trade, destroyed by fire, lost at sea, melted down for gold.

Museums, Youkhanna said, are only as strong as their doors. Asked what could be done, he replied, "Metal doors, bigger locks."

. . .

How long can anything be expected to last? Museums add centuries of life to artifacts, and perhaps some will make it farther, there is no telling. The idea of posterity is sweet, but we seem to be holding artifacts for now rather than the future. Savor this moment of rare assemblages as if we have come to the end of history and gathered as many pieces as we could.

The next day, I asked Haskell if she would take me to the final layer of occupation at Awat'ovi, the Spanish mission that came just before the fall. We returned to the museum and climbed stairs until we encountered the angle of the roof, where she showed me to a disconcertingly small door. Haskell unlocked it and we ducked into the Metals Room, a repository of medieval items: spears, blades, shields, and long, pointed instruments used during the Crusades to disembowel Muslims and Christians alike. Low, steep-angled ceilings threw the room's dimensions askew. We crouched toward the back, dropping to our knees at a set of drawers. Inside were cubbies from which Haskell removed a small manila envelope labeled "door hinge." She poured it out on a sheet of white paper. All that was left were flakes of rust and powder.

"I guess that's a door hinge," she said.

I was surprised to see so little intact material, but considering that the artifact came from a sacked mission that had burned down and was left to weather for a couple of centuries, this was not bad. If it had been higher priority, the museum would have kept the hinge's remains in a plastic container, but this was only one tiny industrial object tipped into an envelope, holding just enough shape for me to see that it had once been a fixture. Every envelope Haskell opened contained something similar: buckle, latch, bolt. The Hopi gave the Peabody murals, pots, and turquoise jewelry, while the Spanish offered rust.

Then something solid appeared. She slipped a coin-sized metal disk from its envelope onto paper. I reached out to turn it over.

"Ah!" Haskell stopped my bare hand. "Skin oils," she warned.

She used the edge of the paper to flip over the disk, revealing a corroded but recognizable image of Christopher, patron saint of lost travelers. The medal had been found on the floor of the mission, and I wondered who had been the last to hold it before it was uncovered by the Peabody's expedition. I was transported to Awat'ovi, to the attack at dusk, just as the sky began filling with stars. As shouts and screams poured through the pueblo, I imagined Anglo missionaries understanding how big a mess they had gotten themselves into. I saw the medal clutched to the breast of a man with eyes wide in horror, praying for his life, hearing shouts and pounding on the wooden doors. Then the doors would have crashed open as warriors broke through, blowing out the candles.

Is there any better justification for a museum's existence than allowing lost worlds to come back to life like this? Time is reborn here. In this confounding room, with its peculiar ceiling and its weapons, I had found the end of my inquiry. I had witnessed the long life and sudden death of a magnificent pueblo, a place I previously knew only as mounds of dust and broken pottery at the edge of a mesa, a place where I had longed to know what had been in the ground.

As Haskell slid the pendant back into its envelope, I thanked her. Then I thanked her again, hoping she would understand my gratitude for her devotion, for holding the memory of this pueblo together when it was not even hers to begin with.

I walked in an evening rain back to my rented room just off campus, where I shook off my raincoat and lay down on the stiff single bed, hands behind my head. I had spent two days sorting through the Peabody. Seeing those murals, pots, and archived photos of men digging trenches in the 1930s—men who have all probably died by now—made the rain sound different, as if it were prying apart the stone tiles on the roof. I was keenly aware of water-fat ivy creeping up the walls of this two-story brownstone, big, green hands pressing against my window as if waiting to get in. I let the house fall apart in my imagination, followed dutifully by the city around it and the rest of the East Coast, leaving only overgrown hills of ruins, streetlamps slumped over like bones, as gone as Awat'ovi. Would there be anyone to excavate our fallen civilization after that, and what would they do with us? Would they snatch at relics and argue?

Would they find the astonishing remains of the Peabody and its artifacts from around the world and think it a place of ancestor worship? Would they be wrong?

I once asked Anibal Rodriguez, a charismatic curator at the American Museum of Natural History in New York, what would become of his museum in a thousand years. Standing in the silent corridors of the Southwest Collection, where he had been working for more than forty years, Rodriguez considered the question and wondered whether there would still be museums.

"Maybe the remains and collections of you and me," he postulated. "By then, the collections you and I are now looking at will have gone home." Gone home. It was a curious notion, as if there were places artifacts would return to, each one having an invisible X to which it belonged, a door it would someday knock on, announcing, *I'm back*.

Listening to the rain in Cambridge, I imagined artifacts picked up one by one and taken to the home Rodriguez spoke of, perhaps even dug out of the rubble of some future Peabody, murals returning to their naked kivas as a gold jar moves into the wild barrancas of the Sierra Madre. A gray jar goes onto the floor of a buried room where it once was romanced by a tree root. The Euphronios ambles to the countryside near San Antonio di Cerveteri. A handful of tiny white beads scatter across the floor of a rock shelter in the desert, as thousands of manuscripts go back to their cave at the edge of the Taklamakan. A story fits back together, one we have guarded and fought over for centuries, one we have torn to pieces in our enthusiasm and sense of entitlement.

There is a rule we are taught from an early age: put things back when you are done. There is no need for us to rush to do this. We have nothing but time.

PART FOUR

IN SITU

CHAPTER 13

NO PLACE LIKE HOME

It matters where things are; stories are told differently as they get shuffled from one place to another. A statue in a museum guarded by a motion detector is not that same statue in a shrine with its feet being kissed off. Moving it under a roof may give us a new past to revel in, but at least consider the equal and opposite reaction: what has happened to the thing that has been lost?

Cornelius Holtorf, a controversial archaeologist at the University of Lund, in Sweden, rattled the scientific community in 2007 by proposing that the past is actually a renewable resource, and we are not being robbed of it. Holtorf, who believes we are not losing sites but actually gaining them, writes, "It has become cliché to lament the loss of ancient sites and objects in the modern Western world in much the same way as we do the continuous reduction of the tropical rainforests and the gradual decline of remaining oil reserves." He says that remnants of the past are not depleted in the same way as environmental resources because we are actually creating more of them: "No other societies have surrounded themselves with as many archaeological sites and objects that can be experienced in the landscape or as part of collections as our modern Western societies." We establish museums and parks dedicated to archaeology, all the while honing tools to look at the past with an ever-sharper eye, finding even more layers to peel back. While I agree with Holtorf's assessment, there is more to the story. We may be making more archaeology all the time, but once the original context is lost, that story is over.

When China last invaded Tibet in the mid-twentieth century, it went to great pains to erase people's physical connection to the past by removing and often destroying their artifacts. So many statues and pieces of religious regalia were hauled out by caravans of transport trucks and melted down that one foundry in Beijing produced six hundred tons of gold bullion of Tibetan ancestry. The People's Liberation Army reduced an original presence of more than six thousand monasteries to thirteen. Ancient libraries of religion, medicine, history, and philosophy were shelled, burned, and rolled over by tanks. Reliquaries of artifacts dating back centuries if not thousands of years were destroyed.

When the political climate began changing in the mid-1980s and surviving cultural objects were made available, delegates sent to China found warehouses and halls filled nearly to their ceilings. In one visit alone they packed up more than thirteen thousand mangled, hammer-beaten statues that they returned to Tibet to let the past back in.

One statue received different treatment, however. It was the Jowo Shakymuni, the most revered object in all Tibet. When the Chinese invaded, this item was on the short list of things that must be left undamaged. Positioned in the center of Lhasa, it is considered the geographic bull's-eye of Tibetan Buddhism, the very axis on which the universe is said to turn. When it arrived in Lhasa in the seventh century as a gift from China, the statue ushered Buddhism into the country. It was the dowry of a Chinese princess steeped in Buddhism who married a powerful Tibetan king, a political and religious alliance that united the two countries. In this most recent invasion, the statue remained unharmed because even after nine hundred years it is still a claim China has put on Tibet, a justification that says, *We brought you Buddhism, now pay up.*

Ancient objects have this kind of power. Leaving them in place is more than just a political gesture. They represent a continuum of active history that affects everyday lives. To this day pilgrims travel hundreds of miles, kissing the ground at every step, to greet the Jowo Shakymuni, and when they arrive in Lhasa they join a procession walking a wide, clockwise circle around the temple that houses it. The circle spirals inward, crimson robes bustling together into a darkened hall where the Jowo glows with a smooth-skinned alloy of gold and silver, the jewels of its robe brilliant in the smoky light.

Had the statue been taken, a substitute probably would have been installed so that the circle would keep turning. This has happened before. There is little chance that today's version is the original Jowo Shakymuni made in India around 560 BC and blessed by the Buddha himself, then later exported to China and finally to Tibet. Lhasa has been sacked many times since the statue first arrived, and though it was probably hidden a few times, somewhere along the line it was likely lost to war or to unscrupulous or forgetful hands, whereupon a new Jowo took its place. What matters most is that there is not a blank spot at the center of this universe. A direct line to the past is still there, embodied by something physical. Placement matters.

I think back to the man who built a replica of a prehistoric loom and put it in the cave in Utah where the original had been. It was strangely haunting for him to know something important was gone, a vacancy that had to be filled.

In Scotland there is a revered seven-ton rock called the

Cadboll Stone, artfully inscribed head to toe, from the ninth century. When the British Museum took it in 1921, locals were in an uproar. They demanded that it be returned, contending that it was part of who they were, and they at least succeeded in getting it moved closer to home, where it can now be seen at the Museum of Scotland, in Edinburgh. A handmade replica has been placed on its original site so there is not a glaring vacuum, but locals are still fighting for the real thing, arguing that the stone was "born" there and "grew" there, and that is where it "should" be. They speak of it as a living thing. Siân Jones, head of archaeology at the University of Manchester, has written extensively on the perplexities and challenges surrounding the Cadboll Stone, compiling a series of interviews with locals. One woman said to Jones, "I do feel it's wanting to go back. We've taken it out, disturbed it, we've looked at it....I mean I know it has to have lots of things done to it to preserve it...but I think once it goes back I feel it'll shine on its own."

For some it is a matter of heart. Heart becomes culture. Places become sacred.

While exploring an archaeological site in the highland interior of Guatemala, I once emerged from the forest onto an ancient plaza. It was a late Mayan city, ruins thick with trees, the plaza made into a clearing. At the far end were the tumbled remains of a temple, and I noticed a wisp of smoke turning among its stones. Curious, I started toward the smoke, head cocked like a dog hearing a whistle. Someone had built a small fire and then smothered it. When I got there I crouched and waved my hand over the scorched circle. It had been snuffed out minutes before my arrival. Around it were arrayed ropes of melted wax, candles of many colors, and tiny stubs of paper matches that had been burned down to keep the candles lit. Between the temple's crooked building blocks were greasy Catholic votive candles and one freshly severed head of a rooster. The ruffle around the rooster's throat was matted and wet with blood, its gray eyelids closed as if sleeping, eyeballs not yet sunken.

These were the remains of a mourning ceremony in which Mayans mix Catholicism with an ancient and much more local religion. Worshippers had brought flowers, just as the Mayans had brought them a thousand years earlier. There were dead flowers, too, and candles, years of them by the looks of it. Whatever this temple was, people knew it by name and perhaps remembered which god or goddess had once been worshipped in this very place. Maybe they had been coming for centuries. The heat of this doused fire helped me realize that this was not merely an archaeological site, not in the scientific sense. It was a place people came to remember. It mattered that it was still here.

. . .

In 2001, William Saturno went to Guatemala under the auspices of the Peabody Museum and discovered what is now being called the Mayan Sistine Chapel. He found it by accident. His guides were lost in the Petén, unable to get him where he wanted to go, and after a few days by Land Cruiser and eight hours by foot they got him to a ruined city that had already been discovered and thoroughly looted. The site looked like a war zone, with trenches burrowed this way and that into jungle-covered temples. Many of the digs were fresh, bright spoil piles of plaster dumped across the ground.

Frustrated, exhausted, and out of drinking water, Saturno entered a looter's trench looking for shade. The trench led to the base of a temple, where it disappeared into darkness. Saturno pulled his flashlight and was stunned to see a portion of a subterranean mural accidentally exposed by tomb raiders. Not only did the mural appear to be intact, but its style looked very old; in fact, it would turn out to be the oldest Mayan mural ever discovered. Saturno later said, "In Western terms, it's like knowing only modern art and then stumbling on a Michelangelo or a Leonardo."

He immediately hired guards to protect the site. The looter's tunnel had undercut the mural's foundation and left a painted wall suspended in midair, so he moved in sand bags and polyester mesh, and installed vertical supports.

Closer examination showed that there were probably a number of large and intact mural panels buried in dirt. Immediately there were cries to excavate, but Saturno held off. A less farsighted archaeologist might have gone straight for the heart and begun ticking away with a trowel on the spot. Instead, Saturno took two years to organize a project, securing grants and specialists. He went so far as to take out personal loans to cover costs. Although curiosity was killing him and many others, he moved not even a fingernail of rock out of the way. Even more than he ached for the dazzle of immediate discovery, he wanted the place preserved for full understanding.

Once he announced that he was going to start excavation, the money came through. Saturno called these the "gravy days." Detail crews rebordered fragile mural edges with lime plaster to prevent further decay. Fallen fragments were reattached, while the remains of destroyed murals — tens of thousands of pieces broken by Mayans themselves in ancient construction episodes — were carried outside and temporarily glued back together in a lab.

What the team unearthed was astonishing: an elegant and beautifully stylized depiction of a creation ceremony from around 200 BC. Starting on the west wall, four deities stand in fabulous headdresses, each god shown bleeding profusely from his own sacrificial wounds as he makes offerings to the cardinal directions: first a dead fish on a burning pyre, then a deer cut open and bleeding from the mouth, followed by a turkey in a similar state of butchery, and finally a sacrifice of fragrant blossoms set ablaze. Continuing down the panel, one sees a corn god establishing the center of the universe upon which all circumstance must turn, and the last scene, a Mayan king ascending to godhood with name, title, and exact date written clearly in glyphs as if stamped with a block. Nothing like it had ever been seen before. It was a glimpse into the birth of Mayan cosmology.

Saturno decided that the murals needed to be left in place, a markedly different approach from that taken at Awat'ovi sixty-five years earlier, when murals were stripped from Arizona using burlap and resin. He told me, "Not only was it serendipitous the way I found them, but it was serendipitous they were found by me."

Indeed, Saturno did everything he could to secure the murals, and after that, he did nothing. He had been schooled in the careful ethics of Barbara and William Fash, who worked the Mayan site of Copán in Honduras, where any major artifacts or pieces of architecture pulled out were replaced by molded replicas so there would at least be no blank spots. Conservation, restoration, and reconstruction by archaeologists has become much more commonplace in Central America. It's as if they're responding to the mass destruction that has happened there, either at the hands of looters or earlier archaeologists, or by the jungle. Scientists are beginning to talk about "a holistic approach."

Saturno scoffed at the notion of moving the murals to a secure location elsewhere, as has been done in the past. "If you can find me a better spot," he said, "fine, but there isn't a better spot, a place climate-controlled with an eternal power source not affected by earthquakes. The oldest building in the United States that is still standing is about three hundred fifty years old, and I'm not sold on that kind of longevity. This temple has been here for two thousand years. Beat that."

"What happens to it next?" I asked.

"Hopefully nothing happens next," he said. "Ideally the murals would stay where they are and as they are. But actually achieving nothing means a lot of work, surprising amounts of work."

Keeping something where it is is a much more active process than simply taking. Guards have to be posted on-site and environmental fluctuations monitored. New support walls must be built, which Saturno plans to do by quarrying limestone from where the Mayans themselves quarried it, using only local lime plaster so that no foreign materials are introduced. His approach involves connectivity rather than removal and isolation. What Saturno has accomplished is a delicate feat, scientific inquiry balanced on the value of a thing in its place.

. . .

The jungle devours ruins. You can walk through a fallen city with hundred-foot temples without ever knowing. Everything here crawls. The canopy buzzes, hums, and drips. Plants attack each other; parasites and chemical invaders suck nitrogen from each other's roots and trunks. Bromeliads hang like sea creatures. This is no museum, no collector's living room. It is the very place where archaeology happened, Mayan civilization at its height.

I stumbled through the root-bridled entropy of the Petén a mere hour from the nearest dirt road, my boots snared in fallen vines, a satchel over my shoulder with a bit of lunch and water. It seemed as if I'd fallen into an abyss. I was traveling through a lowland *bajo* in the eastern part of the country, looking for the remains of an unexcavated Mayan settlement. I was not trying for anything near Saturno's find;

I just wanted to see something of the old Maya still in place. If there was any sort of trail, I was unaware of it. A machete would have been handy—though cumbersome and tiring to swing—for cutting the sloppy shape of my desire through plants. Likely I'd just have hurt myself.

I had been visiting excavated sites in the area, bright limestone temples and pyramids shaved like poodles of their vegetation, but I wanted to know what they looked like in their natural state of decay. There were outlying compounds of structures around here, but I could not find a damn thing but vines and strangled trunks, no horizon to be seen. Sunlight penetrated in slivers.

Lurching this way and that, my limbs snarled, I looked up and suddenly there it was: a shaggy temple place before me, topping out just beneath the canopy, trees grown from its head like a crown. I had to peer at it for a moment to make sure it really was what I thought. This was not a soaring pyramid like those you might see at the nearby Mayan city of Tikál, nor was it miraculously exposed. It was a steep, lonely protuberance blanketed in jungle.

When I drew closer I saw faint pits, shallow holes put down by looters decades ago. The perimeter of this place was watched over by armed guards. No major looting has hit the immediate area in a while. In the rest of the Petén, however, tomb raiders have excavated tunnels into every temple. Grotesque mouths belch spoil piles bright white from lime plaster dug out of building interiors. One archaeologist working in the area told me that pretty much everything in the Petén has been looted.

Looking at the relatively minimal damage to the temple before me, I realized it was possible that there was still an intact tomb inside.

There are two very different ways of seeing what is buried inside a temple. One involves recording the bounce-back rate of subatomic particles, which can make an increasingly detailed internal map (the technique has been employed to study the interior of a pre-Aztec pyramid in the Valley of Mexico without disturbing the site). The other is the old-fashioned way: digging your way in, swinging metal tools over your shoulder.

Let's say you were a digger in Guatemala and you found this temple. You would put two or three short tunnels made of cockeyed limestone blocks into a clump of overgrowth and find nothing but architectural fill and a smattering of cheap, broken artifacts. Maybe on the fourth try you would hit a smooth slab, the inner wall of a tomb. Picking out a seam and breaking through, you would reach an interior vault where you would have to clear away fallen rubble, which would then open onto a seated skeleton enshrined in shells, pottery, vessels, and jade adornments.

A looter coming upon this site would quickly survey the immediate area, knowing that if there is one temple, there are probably many others. Most often, these temples are formally arranged around a cardinal axis, and those on the north side tend to produce the richer tombs, a by-product of Mayan cosmology.

It might have been enough to stand beside this monument of vegetation and recognize it for what it was—eighth-century Late Classic Mayan architecture succumbed—but I wanted to get to its crest. I started climbing. In a way, it was sheer vanity that drove me up the side, my desire to get as close as I could to a very long time ago, just to see what it felt like. At least at the larger temples, there used to be human sacrifices up top. Evidence of iron and albumen soaked into stucco floors at certain sites suggests they were once awash in blood. One could imagine sacrificial victims struggling up blood-slick steps to reach the top, where they would have been laid across a stone altar, bare chests aimed up into the thrust of an obsidian blade. That in itself was reason to climb.

A smaller temple, this one probably saw less-dramatic sacrifices. There may have been decapitations of turkeys up here or the burning of fragrant herbs, maybe a tad of royal bloodletting on special days. The Mayans were not nearly as grim as the Aztecs to the north who followed them. An archaeologist once told me of sitting on one of the great Aztec temples, slapping mosquitoes on a limestone altar. He said the mosquitoes were engorged with his blood, and he was enchanted by the bridge built in his mind, his blood and that of ancients there on the same stone. Maybe it's just sympathetic magic, maybe it's not even real, but it sure feels tangible.

Building my own bridge to the past, I ascended the temple's side, shirt matted against my skin. Insect urine fell from the canopy in a gentle, continuous drizzle. I was not imagining sacrificial bodies tumbling down the steps around me Aztec style. Here I saw a man alone, ascending clean limestone steps, a bundle of ceremonial items in his hands as he climbed to make an offering. Perhaps he had come some distance on a pilgrimage, and maybe like me he was on his hands and knees owing to the steepness of this temple. It was like climbing a ladder, roots and tumbled limestone blocks filthy and pitted with erosion. The thing had more or less been turned into a forest, and I was gripped by the awareness of civilizations abandoned and falling back into the ground.

Hands reaching ahead, carefully grabbing trunks to pull myself up, I came to an upper platform enclosed by broken-down walls, which was more or less the top. To go any higher I would have to climb on unstable pillars, so I plunked down in a bed of humus to catch my breath. Sunlight winked through the canopy onto my shoulders. Ants came and went, making busy commerce of the site. I crawled along their teeming trail behind this altar chamber, moving over roots and crooked stones. It was a sort of foyer, with only one way in and out. The ornately carved altar that probably once stood here was gone, as were stone facings covered in glyphs that would have borne the names and dates of those who ruled here or the wars they made, now perhaps in a museum vault or standing against a wall in a Fifth Avenue apartment. How much more powerful they would be if they were still here, presiding over this civilization and its continual fall.

At the top of the temple I sat listening to the stillness, not a breeze in this place. Only the tinkering of insects said anything about the movement of time. I was back inside the altar chamber, thinking that a shaman-priest must once have stood on this spot, right where my feet were, looking across great ceremonies of fire and blood. Throngs of men and women would have gathered below, with glittering hair ornaments and turquoise beads stabbed into their noses. The audience would have been decked out in jaguar robes and feathered banners; traders, growers, and architects all in attendance. Trees would have been felled long before, the ground pounded hard and chalky white from limestone cutting. I could have seen this nowhere else.

James O. Young points out that Stonehenge was once for sale. "It would have been a travesty," he said, "had an American tycoon bought it and had it relocated to Druidworld in Florida."

Though it is remarkable to walk into the actual Egyptian Temple of Dendur at the Met, or step out across the London Bridge that was transported stone by stone to Lake Havasu City, Arizona, they seem perfectly out of place. It is a different experience to know you are in the original location. The air feels charged. Maybe it is historicity, all in the mind, but the mind makes it real. Like the Jowo Shakymuni or the

Cadboll Stone, objects take on a unique power when they are in situ. Holtorf is absolutely right in saying that we are creating more past all the time—but it's not this past, and not this place.

I peered through what straight lines were left in the temple's architecture onto a world where a priest once paraded in a jeweled headdress past his subjects, listening to their cries, watching his civilization slowly fall. And as I watched, the jungle seemed to be closing in tighter, finishing its kill.

~~~~~~~~~~

CHAPTER 14

HOLDING ON

Connections with the past are not always maintained in place. Some artifacts are in motion, flying from hand to hand with no actual home to return to. You've got to practically race to keep up with them.

A private collector in Santa Fe named Forrest Fenn is a cheerleader for the right of anyone to get his hands on the past and carry it with him. Fenn has enough money to make a multimillion-dollar go at his obsession, turning his house into a museum.

I visited Fenn when he was seventy-eight, a jovial, gray old man, not very tall but neatly dressed. He made his money from the Santa Fe art market, selling art and antiquities to so many of the rich and famous that he became a *People* magazine celebrity twenty years ago. Now he had a softness about him, an exciting innocence. As he moved with a wobbly shuffle through his remarkable collection of antiquities, I could see that age had caught up with him. He must have been goblinlike in younger years, his limbs and face still ripe with enthusiasm. He showed me a number of ornate bronze canisters he had had cast, planning to bury them around the world with his memoirs sealed inside. He wants someone to dig up his story. One of the bronzes is actually a bell on which he has indelibly inscribed, *If you should ever think of me a thousand years from now, please ring my bell so I will know*. It is kind of like freezing your head after you die, but with an archaeological twist. The cherry on top, Fenn grinned, was that the tongue inside the bell came from a seventeenth-century Spanish mission bell.

"Save the past for the future?" Fenn boasted. "When is the future? Give me a date."

As a collector, Fenn has made himself conspicuous and been outspoken. He likes to argue with archaeologists because, as he says, "they are so easy." (I have heard the same said of him.) There are a good number of archaeologists who would not stop to help Fenn if his car had broken down on the side of the road. He just has that effect on them. (He once held a barbecue for a group of Pueblo Indians and archaeologists, and after they began eating he told them he had grilled their burgers on charcoal excavated from an ancient New Mexico ruin. According to Fenn, the Indians grinned, as they often do when amused by Anglo irony, while the archaeologists just went pale.)

Years back, he bought a piece of land on which stood a huge ruined pueblo, his sole purpose being to excavate at his leisure. He has taken about 1 percent of it, which amounts to the emptying of around thirty rooms. Because it sits on private property, he can do as he wishes. In public hands this would be considered a major American archaeological site, a multithousand-room pueblo occupied from pre-Columbian times up to the installation of a Spanish mission. In Fenn's hands, some consider it a catastrophe.

There are those who would have him shut down in a heartbeat. They have used aerial photos of his digs to try to legally force him to stop, which failed. One government land agent wrote an interagency memo that stated: "The best action would be to somehow get the property into federal or state ownership so it could be better protected. Land exchange or purchase could be possible by the BLM. The bad publicity by the lawsuits could entice Fenn to give up his property." Fenn responded with lawsuits of his own, and he kept digging.

(A few weeks after my visit, Fenn's house was raided by federal agents. They walked out with his files, computers, and a handful of artifacts, but Fenn's antiquities are so well provenanced that they got what he sees as next to nothing. And he has the legal savvy to make sure they won't come back for more.)

Fenn self-published a thick book on his finds from the pueblo he purchased and has done a surprisingly fine job of curating the artifacts down to the potsherd-and-charcoal level. The site has its own room in his house, as neatly drawered and labeled as any public collection. He explained that he is not interested in sloppy work; he wants it done right. He goes to archaeologists for help with identification or for suggestions on conservancy techniques. When he digs into something fragile or important—say, a cache of painted wooden masks—he asks archaeologists if they would come and make sure nothing is damaged. A few have responded. Most, however, consider it professional suicide to be caught working shoulder to shoulder with Forrest Fenn.

But Fenn, as I discovered, is not the enemy they would like him to be. In his own way, and very successfully, he has worked to bridge the gap of time. In a personal fashion, he is reconnecting stories to objects, doing very much what researchers are striving for, only in a way they never could, or would.

. . .

Fenn's house in Santa Fe is a personal museum. With its steel vault and its decorated halls, it is a tour through the ages, bits of Pompeii and Chaco, statues on pedestals, painted skulls, rugs, and Indian robes on the walls (one Plains skin bears a bullet hole, and the hole has been sewed up with beads after the fact, as if closing off a mortal wound). Wanting it all to be seen, he invites strangers like me into his halls. The day I was there, he left me alone in a room crowded with pure gold and silver gewgaws centuries old. There was a jade mask of Olmec origin one might be tempted to lift up and wear, surreptitiously putting on a dead man's face just to see what it felt like. When Fenn returned he noticed me lingering at the mask.

"Try it on if you want," he said.

I laughed nervously, said no, thank you. Fenn shrugged. "I don't especially like it. I got it about five years ago so I could trade it for something I really want to play with."

One thing Fenn is is honest. He plays with these things. No words are minced. He used to sell fake antiquities, and he admitted up front what he was doing even as other dealers accused him of poisoning the market. He could not care less.

"This!" he announced as he picked up a tarnished silver bracelet with inlaid turquoise beads. "This is the bracelet Richard Wetherill had made after he discovered Cliff Palace—when was it?—1888! And these twenty-two beads are the very ones he collected that day!" Wetherill had gone on to work with Gustaf Nordenskiöld at Mesa Verde. Like a happy wizard, Fenn shoved the bracelet into my hands. He wanted me to adore it. Everything he touched had some story. There were even two flattened soda cans, the kind you might find on the street, hung on the wall along with pre-Columbian artifacts. Fenn lifted one off its nail, commenting on the rarity of such a perfectly flat can. It was nearly as thin as paper.

"I can relate to this can," he said. "Somebody's driving

down the street drinking a Coca-Cola, they throw the can out on Galisteo Street right downtown, five hundred cars run over it, and it turns into this, like a little piece of art. It's kind of a metaphor for a person's life. It has history in it. If I knew who bought this can, how much they gave for it, where they got it, when they drank it, when they threw it out, I would write a story."

When you start looking around Fenn's collection, when you get behind the glare of premier artifacts, you begin to see an undercurrent of smaller, personal histories that speak to his obsession. There is a 50-mm shell that he said misfired when he was a fighter pilot in Vietnam, the brass chewed up when it flew into his intake. And among those objects of gold and silver, you'll find a sturdy pair of sandals made from black tire tread. He said he got them from a Viet Cong prisoner. "I traded him a package of cigarettes right through the concertina wire. He took them off and handed them to me. He was a nice guy, he was just the enemy."

"You've got this deep need to gather things," I said.

"Information," Fenn replied. "It's not the object, it's the story behind the object."

Fenn rattled out a small plastic box filled with brass tacks. "These came from a conquistador. I was getting gas twenty miles this side of Cody, Wyoming, when this truck pulled up and everybody was gathered around looking at what was in the bed. I went over and they had a conquistador and his horse—everything, the bones, armor, chain mail, all the horse trappings. They found it eroding out of an arroyo. Now, I don't think conquistadors were supposed to be up that far, but there's your story. I asked, if you let me crawl back there and pick up those tacks, would you let me keep them? They said yes."

He picked up one of the tacks between thumb and forefinger. It was as small as the butt of a pen. "See the square shank? It's the real thing. Here, I'll give you one." Before I could figure out whether to say yes or no, he popped it into a small plastic specimen bag and handed it to me. "Here you go. Treat it with respect, it's very historical."

He said, "Every time I drive through that town I stop. There's a little museum where I ask if anyone knows anything about that old conquistador, and nobody does. It's gone. Who knows, I might be the only one who remembers the story." He gestured at the bag, which I had already tucked into my shirt pocket. "Now you know it, too."

Fenn is like a bag lady shambling ahead through time, carrying all the past he can collect, sprinkling it into the pockets of passersby. He is a transporter. But not only of objects; he is moving stories along with them, bringing them back to light in the glow of his own enthusiasm. He writes everything down—the gas station where he got the conquistador's tacks (Meeteetse, Wyoming) and details of a card game in which he won Wetherill's bracelet. These are the stories often lost to the laundering process as dealers and collectors scrub out the past so it won't be incriminating. Meanwhile, Fenn marvels over the entire testimony, every hand along the way. He does not believe in laundering. He sees what researchers often do not, that an artifact's history does not end when it falls into the ground. Granted, he treats the past very differently from, say, Bill Saturno, who left his mural discovery in place, but he has a completely different version of what it is right to do.

Said Fenn, "I can't tell you how many thousand times I've been digging and I found something, an arrowhead, four feet deep. You know what I tell myself? My Lord, how pleased this thing is to be looking at the sun again after being down there in hell. I liberated it. It was made to look at and to use. When you find something like that out there, isn't it just begging you to take it?"

"No," I said, thinking of the ground more as a place to sleep on than as hell.

"It's not talking to you?" he asked, incredulous.

"I think that's the sound of you begging yourself to take it."

"It's not talking to you?" he asked again, as if he could not believe my answer. "Here's what it's saying to you. It's saying, *Craig, if you don't pick me up and take me home and love me, Joe Smith is going to find me tomorrow and sell me for twenty-five bucks.*"

"I know," I said. "But Joe Smith has to figure it out for himself."

"Let me show you something." He walked across the floor of his vault and lifted a display box containing an elaborate wooden pipe, its long stem spiraling into a red soapstone bowl.

"You know what this is?" Fenn asked. "Sitting Bull's pipe."

I puzzled for a moment, questions flying into my head. *How did you get this? Is it real? It should be in the Smithsonian, or in the hands of the Sioux. It is a national treasure. What are you going to do with it?* My thoughts distilled into disbelief.

"Are you serious?" I asked. "That's Sitting Bull's actual pipe? You've got *Sitting Bull's pipe?*"

"This is arguably one of the most important American Indian artifacts in existence," Fenn said. "There's no way it isn't the original pipe. It's exact. I even measured the concavities in the bowl itself. The ratios are perfect."

He had also, he would later explain, compared digitally enhanced pictures of the wood grain to 1883 photos of the grain on the actual pipestem (Sitting Bull was often photographed holding it). The grain matched perfectly. A number of collectors and keepers have claimed to have the original, but this one is almost impossible to refute. It is indeed Sitting Bull's pipe, the one that belonged to the Lakota Sioux holy man and warrior, his tool of intimacy and diplomacy. Fenn said it had come out of a mom-and-pop museum in Minnesota, where the owners had had it for thirty years without ever knowing what it was. A trader recognized it and picked it up. Fenn asked if he could hold on to it just to prove that it wasn't the real thing. When he realized it was, he bought it.

I asked, "Do you...touch it?"

"Oh yeah, you want to touch it?" Fenn said, opening the case, lifting out the age-slicked wood, its mid- and foresections decorated with rings of brass caps. "You can touch it. I want you to feel the hand polish on it, the velvetness of it."

I cradled the pipe, the stem nearly as long as my forearm. The coolness went out of the wood as my hands moved over its surface, oiled from more than a century of touch. I saw in this object the sparkling flare of photographers illuminating the face of Sitting Bull as he posed with this very object in his hands, a man who in his youth knocked a Crow warrior off a horse and took his father's name, who one day handed this pipe to his son, One Bull. I saw the Indian Wars, and Custer going down in Sitting Bull's dream, and then in his reality. I heard General Phil Sheridan's infamous rejoinder, "The only good Indians I ever saw were dead."

I listened to the pipe's wood for a cold, rainy morning, December 15, 1890, when two shots were fired by police, one into Sitting Bull's side, the next into his head, finally toppling this legend from his horse.

"Would you have left this, too?" Fenn demanded. "Would you have walked away from it if you found it somewhere?"

No, I wanted to say. Yes. My God, it was beautiful.

"Why shouldn't we be able to touch this?" he pressed.

"What is wrong with giving you this feeling? It is a privilege."

I was astonished that it was here at all, that the pipe had survived wars and uncountable years when it must have moved through many hands, often at risk of disappearing. How long would this have gone on before the connection of memory broke forever, leaving another of the countless shadows with nothing to cast it? It was not luck that brought the pipe to Fenn, a man who, if nothing else, could tie the loose ends of time back together. Fenn had been looking for it all along. While private collectors tend to be vilified for destroying history, without Fenn, the pipe's connection to Sitting Bull might have been lost.

Where might it go from here? Who could know? Fenn said it was a question he asked himself ten million times, and he had no answer, no institution or heir picked out. It was as if all he could see was the pipe's past, the future a mystery he did not care to unravel. This is where he ultimately wanted it, in his possession, where a person could hold it, taking in history with all his senses. At least now the world knows where Sitting Bull's pipe was in the summer of 2009: in my hands.

CHAPTER 15

~~~~~~~~~~

LETTING GO

I have my own private collection that spans the American Southwest in its tiers of canyons and sharp-sided mesas. A gray ceramic olla lies upside down like a helmet in Arizona beneath a needle-tip peak, and three hundred miles away in a cave a pair of Apache water baskets are seated in a nest of wood-rat droppings. A painted clay canteen rests on its side under a sandstone band shell in southeast Utah, one horizon north of a red seed jar off in the shade of a boulder. In between are three wooden knife handles of Anasazi origin, sanded and stacked and ready for stone blades to be inserted and bound with sinew, waiting there for someone who never came. My landscape is a map of objects like these, compass points and ancient benchmarks found among the dust and spiderwebs of ten thousand cracks.

"They are just objects," a friend said to me. "They can't have been that important if somebody left them there."

But objects stretch beyond their physical boundaries. Their character lies in their placement on the earth, the way they are set down by hand or dropped from a pouch. This is provenance at its best.

An archaeologist once told me that because I would not reveal the locations of artifacts I had found in situ, I was no better than a common vandal. He protested that I was dooming my finds to looters by leaving them unidentified and unresolved. As we sat in his office, his computer like a big blue eye behind him, he did not seem bitter about this, just mystified. I shrugged uncomfortably, feeling as much at a loss for words as the day Ugly Man had stolen the bow.

I said, "I think they're fine as they are."

"And if they are taken?"

"That's the risk."

"Risk for what purpose?"

For the place and for the artifacts themselves. Our ravening fingers have lifted almost every last hidden thing. My pursuit of artifacts had so far been my business alone, a preoccupation with discovery and antiquity, and the least I could do after I found them was leave them be.

I said none of this to the archaeologist. Instead, I merely told him that since I was the one who found them, I got to decide. Finders keepers, you know. In Greece you are required by law to report finds as, say, you dig skeletons and vases out of your basement while doing plumbing repairs. But not in the United States. Here it is still legal to walk away and say nothing.

I have never marked these artifacts on any maps. This is not out of secrecy or for fear someone will abscond with my maps and snap up every bread crumb I found. I simply figure that I will remember the way. If I don't, problem solved. They slip back into oblivion. I am in love with the fate of artifacts, especially when they pass beyond our reach, and only rarely do I return to these sites.

An exception is a crackerjack basket that lies deep inside the wildly eroded geography of the Colorado Plateau. The basket is of a style dating back 1,500 years, and it waits there like a prize. A person can reach it only by crossing a buckled canyon in the high desert, something out of an epic tale—

ledges and pitfalls, sandstone dragons guarding their keep. The dominant rock formation, Wingate sandstone, is the color of dried blood, and it breaks away into blocks several hundred feet tall. In its perfectly vertical state, this formation is a bitch to navigate unless you know a route. I know one.

. . .

I was out with Regan in late October. We were way out of range of pothunters; people can't even get in here by helicopter. We crept down a bedrock face, hands reaching to each other, packs lowered on a sixty-foot tether. I was coming to get a sample from the basket for carbon-14 dating. I needed just a little nip. An archaeologist had expressed interest, so I said I would return with a piece, as long as no location was revealed.

I thought I knew the route but it was deceptive, my recollection not as keen as I had hoped. It had been several years. I led us out onto a ledge as wide as a diving board, but it quickly whittled down to the width of a two-by-four. Regan was standing at my heels looking around my shoulder.

"Wrong way?" she asked.

I stared at the ledge in front of me, which tapered to a teaspoon handle. The earth gaped below, four hundred feet of ledges and free fall.

Interpreting my dumbfounded silence, Regan turned before I did, her shoulders brushing against the cliff face as she set off looking for a better route.

"I think there's a way back here," she said.

I remained at the lip, with my eyes fixed on the exposure.

"Yeah," she called back. "Here it is, over here."

I turned and looked for her, but she was gone, already on the way down.

My misdirection had lost us about half an hour, long enough to screw the rest of the day. It got late, orange shafts of sun cutting into the canyons below as the shadow of our cliff leaned across the earth. Half an hour of backtracking was too long. Dark was coming, and we needed at least two hours to reach the next stage of land below. Regan cracked a half smile when our situation became obvious.

"Let's find a place to sleep," I said.

Easier said, of course: we were on a crag-faced rock several hundred feet tall. The only possibility was a ledge where a chunk of wall had fallen away. You could lie on it lengthwise, but your arm would hang over. Good enough. Getting there required a small commitment, a step over an abyss ending on a tiny clip of rock—not something to attempt while wearing a pack. Regan stepped across without hers, her boot sole landing perfectly, hands against the rock to hold her steady. She turned to me as I unloaded our packs, handing belongings across.

That evening I cooked noodles in a small pan with easy turns of a spoon, my legs folded beneath me. Regan was sitting on her sleeping bag, leaning on her palm while light withdrew from the canyons below. She and I had camped many places in our lives, but never together at a vista so serene and so violent, two feet of flat, several hundred feet of vertical. The ledge sharpened our awareness, forcing us to think before making a move. Do not set down a pen or a journal; do not stand up quickly.

An evening-cool breeze swept across us as we crawled into sleeping bags head to toe. I placed a rock under my left hip, a little reminder not to roll in my sleep.

I have never slept so well, so beautifully, as that night. You have sound dreams on a ledge, still as a mummy, hands crossed on your chest. It was like being suspended by a silver thread over the desert. In the first light of morning I woke refreshed as Regan prepared tea with great care. We sat side by side, sipping and watching the sun rise below us, our legs in sleeping bags as we dangled our bones over the edge, the basket way down there.

. . .

I originally found this basket while traveling with three companions. I had pulled off my hat and stuck my head in a crack to see if anything was there. Noticing a dim shape, I reached back and touched the curve of it. We took it out, photographed it, spent a couple of days sketching and admiring it, then put it back, with no mention that we were there.

One person who roams the area around the Colorado River in Utah likes to slide curt little communiqués into artifacts: *You were not the first to find this. Please leave it the way it was when you got here.* Sometimes I am a bit put off when I find this memorandum, this note claiming possession of a site, clearly reading *Mine!* Once I even thought of tearing up a note and returning the place to the way it was before it was found, but I folded the paper and put it back exactly the way it had been. After all, the note writer and I wanted the same thing.

One of the most venerable guardians out here is a man in his late fifties named Fred Blackburn, who has traveled hard in the Four Corners for thirty-five years. Possessor of a gravelly voice, there's a bit of respectable redneck to him. Back in 1974 Blackburn was the first federal ranger at Grand Gulch in Utah, where he battled the black market at a time when drug runners were starting to moonlight as pothunters.

Now long retired from rangering, he leads surveys on the Navajo reservation, carefully choosing which sites to report and which never to mention. The best place for an artifact, he believes, is where it was found, and he does not want to draw unnecessary attention to still pristine locations. Some-times things disappear quickly when word gets out, so he is careful about what he reports.

It is not the black market alone that rankles Blackburn. He is also unhappy with government archaeologists and bureaucrats who have pulled out some prime pieces, ostensi-bly to protect them from being stolen. One artifact he is par-ticularly embittered about is a wooden staff. He found it in an area he was surveying in Utah, a place where he kept coming upon rock art panels showing figures with staffs, their tops curled over like shepherds' crooks.

The staffs — said by some descendants to be objects of power, things that were themselves considered alive — cap-tured his imagination. Blackburn had seen them in muse-ums and in a photograph of pothunter Earl Shumway lying in a burial he'd just emptied, but he had never found one in the field himself until, looking for shade, he climbed back into a broken-down cliff with some of his surveyors.

"I looked down in the crack and there was one of those damn staffs," he said. "Like it was presented to us."

I have actually seen this staff and admired its finely knot-ted wood. It does not look like local wood; maybe it's creo-sote bush from the south (Blackburn wonders if it comes from Mexico). One end is sharpened and worn as if it had frequently been stuck upright in the ground (perhaps with feathers hanging off it), its head flattened and rolled over. Altogether this staff is about four feet long. Smoothed by much touching, it rests in a drawer at the Edge of the Cedars Museum in Blanding, Utah. It is there because after Black-burn reported it, a local Bureau of Land Management archaeologist insisted that it be removed and protected from thieves.

Blackburn seethed as he talked about this episode. "In their panic to preserve they lose half the story. All they're getting is the object itself with a little provenance." People seeing the staff do not naturally know about nearby rock art or the sheltering wall crevice in which it was stashed.

He said the archaeologist on the case wanted only to retrieve the staff after it was reported. Blackburn was even invited along on the expedition to fetch it, but he gave a flat *Hell no*. "It's criminal as far as I'm concerned," he said.

The archaeologist went on to write an exhaustive report on this staff and other finds like it, a stack of paper almost two inches thick that preserves what context she could.

I asked Blackburn if he ever returns to the site.

"No," he retorted bitterly. "Anymore, I stay away from that area. I don't want to go back."

Blackburn has an alternative. He and his field colleagues have proposed what he calls an "outdoor museum." Its premise is simple: leave everything where you find it. That's all. If you want to see it, find it the way everyone else has, by walking. He said he had recently found twelve jars weathered out of a wash together. I asked him what had happened to them, and he said, "They've probably washed away by now." He added, "It's not just about the artifact. I don't think we're mature enough as a nation to understand this yet. We're still in Manifest Destiny mode."

It could be rationally argued that Blackburn's outdoor museum is the most destructive of them all, because it will ultimately result in total obliteration. If artifacts are simply left in the ground, their decay is guaranteed, and if no one else ever sees them, they are forever out of the loop of contemporary understanding. But why must they be in the loop? Must we command every piece of antiquity we encounter? Blackburn argues that there is value in the untrammeled process. His approach allows these artifacts to fade naturally out of existence as we take ourselves out of the equation. This Zen approach makes the hoarding of archaeology seem desperate and reckless. I admire Blackburn's fidelity to natural processes.

. . .

Here is how I would like the story to go: I mentioned our finding the basket to a government archaeologist, who then asked if I could get a sample for him to radio-carbon date, and sent me on this mission.

Here is what really happened: I never personally met the archaeologist. He was alerted to the basket's presence by a couple of buddies of mine who were with me when we found it. They showed him pictures, and he was quite interested, but then bemused when they refused to give an exact location. He responded with a couple of questions and a thank-you. When they recently told him I was heading back into the area and that I would be happy to pick up a sample for dating—another pin to add to his timeline of this region— he said, *Sure.*

The basket was tucked down inside layers of gloriously eroded landscape, one rock formation beneath another. Climbing off the night's bivouac ledge, we reached a black-brush flat far below—finally a horizon to walk on, but it soon fell into a pit of canyons with more cracks to slip down, more jumping for footholds. The next night we spent atop a big mushroom of sandstone, and the next near a spring spat-tering out of a nest of maidenhair ferns.

From the spring we shimmied up a crack, popped through a gap into an isolated canyon on the other side, where we moved along an upper level, eventually entering a hanging side canyon. Inside this side canyon lay the basket. Getting there was like opening a combination lock, turning a key just so.

Just as I had the first time, I got down on one knee, pulled off my hat, and stuck my head in the crack, peering into a dim slot. There was the shape in the back, the basket turned upside down exactly as I had seen it when I was last here. I reached in through strands left by black widows, brushing past pendulums of dangling dead things, and picked up the basket with the tips of my fingers.

It was about the shape of a medium-sized mixing bowl, and it had been used by people in the earliest centuries AD. Its style—yucca strands woven into a nearly watertight coil, with a faint decorative band near the top made from brown-dyed fibers—dates to a cultural era known as Basketmaker. Somebody put it here because he wanted it kept safe, choosing a shelter that let in not even a skim of light, a place that collects less dust than a display case. I held it to the light and slipped it into a silk scarf to keep my skin greases off it. Its inside was hung with a light tracery of spiderwebs that I cleared with two fingers. I handed the basket to Regan, and she cradled it—sturdy enough that you could toss it on a counter and fill it with apples. You'll hardly find such a good basket in a museum.

I think again of Will Tsosie, the Navajo archaeologist from northern Arizona, who once said to me, "In order to be alive, all things must die." He was stating his belief that objects should live out their lives and then be gone. It is a sentiment he shares with Fred Blackburn.

There is something to be said for letting things stay in situ as long as they possibly can, even if it means that a hunter might show up tomorrow and take them, or that they are swallowed by weather. We have no choice but to live among contradictions. If anyone tells you there is only one right answer to the conundrum of archaeology, he is trying to sell you something. At this point, considering all that has been removed, it is worth leaving the last pieces where they lie. As for what is already out of the ground, by all means, move it around, whether you repatriate it or pass it on to the next collector. I'm not proposing anything radical. Don't go to your nearest museum and cut out the glass as I once did, imagining that you can set the world back to the way it once was. That time is over. Let us at least appreciate all that has been gathered, and for the rest, let it lie.

Regan and I took pictures of the basket from various angles, close-ups of its dusty coil weave and the thin, faded band ringing it. We encircled the artifact with a tape measure and marked down a rough circumference of thirty inches. When we were done, I took out a pair of tweezers and twisted off a little piece of frayed material, a small theft. The sample was no bigger than a pencil eraser, just enough for a radioisotope reading. It was a momentary entitlement. I transferred the snippet to a strip of aluminum foil that I folded and slipped into a plastic specimen case.

I picked up the basket, weighed it in my hands once, twice, and reached it back into the crack. It liquefied into the shade, and I let it go.

CODA

I've got this little box of archaeology. It's a Christmas-card box from the 1940s with a snowman on it, cardboard split at the corners as if somebody had stepped on it. It used to be held together by a rubber band, but that grew brittle and broke years ago and has not been replaced, so when I pick up the box it's like trying to move a tray of marbles, with arrowheads and pieces of pottery falling out. Because of that, I don't move it much. It sits on my desk or migrates to a shelf. For a while I kept it in a file drawer. Every few months or so I stumble on it as I'm leafing through a stack of papers or peeling back books, and there it is underneath. I sometimes take off the lid to ponder its contents, either separating out each specimen like a curator or looking at them all at once and wondering, also like a curator, *What am I going to do with these?* Sometimes I even imagine leaving the box somewhere in the wilderness, a pile of lost pieces, a half-assed gesture of repatriation. I won't, though. The box contains polished, grooved stones, and, as I said, arrowheads and potsherds, about forty objects altogether. There is also a clay pipe, its rim blackened from smoking, the same kind of pipe that showed up in the 2009 Four Corners bust, when a guy sold a handful of them for just under $3,000. Probably the best pieces, at least my favorites, are three nearly heart-shaped pendants cut and polished out of black slate, a kind of adornment you would have seen in North America several thousand years ago among big-game hunters. They are similar to the Archaic "bannerstones" more common in the East. Each is notched on one side, so they form different-sized mirrors of each other, and I wonder: Were they all found together? Were they all made at once? Did they come a great distance? I've thought about stringing one and wearing it, but they don't feel as if they are mine to wear. They belong together in a box.

I received the box from my father, and he got it from my grandfather, who got it from my great-grandfather. As far as I can determine, my great-grandfather picked up the various pieces when he was living in southern New Mexico, probably strolling out in the dry grasslands or up at the rocky edges of mountains, shoulders bent, eyes to the ground. He was an inventor, a tinkerer, and held a patent on a kind of oil-lamp burner. When he died, he left a house and a shop in the town of Roswell, and it looked as if he had never thrown away a single thing. There were upholstery tools, radios taken apart, yellow-paged books, boxes of buttons, drawers of wires, windowsills crowded with rocks and sticks. Corridors were carved out of his artifacts with barely enough room to pass through. As a kid I used to be enchanted with his place, spending hours in free-for-all exploration, like Howard Carter cracking open Tut's tomb at every turn. This box of his was one of the few things we saved.

My grandfather died years later, and the box was found in the absurd mess of his garage. When my father died, the box sat in an unoccupied bedroom that looked as if a mad scientist had been living in it for years. Now it travels through my own study, a space crowded with animal skulls, open books, journal articles stacked precariously atop each other, and a stone axe paperweight that Mario gave me in the Sierra Madre. It is difficult for me to part with anything that has a story. Even when a favorite eating bowl breaks, I cannot bear to dump it in the trash, as if it had never contained a piece of my heart. I take the remains into the woods behind my house and I pitch them, potsherds for the future.

I am reminded of an artifact hoard found in a Chicago suburb in the summer of 2009. An old man had died, and his son invited authorities to the home to deal with what looked like up to $10 million in mostly illegally imported artifacts. The FBI went through a living space crowded with boxes stacked five feet high, containing artifacts and documents dating back as far as the fourth century BC. There were parchments and manuscripts from Pope Paul III in the 1500s and Pope Paul V in the 1600s. There were letters from kings, paintings, figurines, sculptures, 3,600 items in all. The son said his father had been traveling to Italy for decades and shipping artifacts home, intending to sell them. But instead of selling, he hung on to the collection. "He fell in love with it, to be honest," the son said. "He thought it was beautiful. He thought it was history." The son believed these artifacts belonged to the world, not to an individual; that schism caused a decade of silence between him and his father.

Once the old man had died (after having personally translated more than a thousand of the manuscripts), his son made sure that the most valuable artifacts went back to their sources. Some 1,600 pieces were turned over to the Italian government. Though they disagreed with each other, father and son ultimately acted together, one reaching back in time to make a connection, the other moving it into the future. A collection that previously did not exist was privately assembled and then made public.

Donny George Youkhanna once told me, "If you want to

send an arrow a far distance, you pull the bow as far back as you can. As much as you know about your ancestors, you send it forward. You must know *what* you have, know *how* it came to you, know *where* it came to you."

My own great-grandfather would have been pleased to know I still have his box, his little hoard carried into the future. He was in love with the world. He wanted to touch it over and over, the same kind of involvement I saw in private collectors who paraded me through their antiquities, and in Haskell leading me through the storied artifacts of the Peabody. I saw it in the undergrad kneeling at the jar she was excavating in Arizona. It was in my father once upon a time, as he crouched on the ground, shotgun leaning against his shoulder as he picked up potsherds, showing me how to appreciate something old and in its place.

My dad lived at the edge of Phoenix. In my teenage years we would take walks together through the desert, finding heaps of abandoned appliances, washing machines rusted and riddled with bullet holes, signs of the oncoming city. People had been leaving junk in the desert for a long time, all the way back to pottery that I would spit on to see if it had any painted design. Together, my dad and I found natural shelters pocked in the sides of dry mountains, where ashen dust contained cooked rabbit bones and lithic scatter, and if we had a finer lens, we would have seen pollens of agave and corn from when the Hohokam farmed this area.

Sometimes my dad would stand in his backyard at night, the bud of his cigarette glowing in his hand as he looked at the city burning bright in the distance. He told me that he saw ghosts dancing out there. It was where the Hohokam used to live, all those graves that salvage archaeologists had yet to reach. I think he really believed he saw them. I think I believed him, too. Maybe it was just the brightness of the oncoming city he saw. Within ten years, the city would surround his house and pass him by, leaving him stranded among four-lanes and diamond-bright car dealerships.

I sometimes wonder what happened to those ghosts, now reduced to pieces of pottery and arrowheads nabbed from the ground, little boxes stuffed with artifacts we keep because we cannot bear forgetting.

. . .

Time was never meant to last. It couldn't. It has no shape. It threads through your fingers like water, no stopping it for any longer than you can cup your palm. Beyond the small memories of our generations, there are artifacts, the substance of history.

Though there is a beauty to letting it go, opening your hand and letting time spill out, I am not immune to a desire that seems to be human through and through: grab something from the past and hang on to it as if it were all there ever was. One cannot fault the desires we have to hold on to these artifacts. But having every last one is overkill. Items become discolored by violation, issues intractable. Problems appear with no solution. This is why I embarked upon this book, looking for an answer.

Where did this journey ultimately lead? To the side of a road in New Mexico near where a salvage archaeologist I know had once cleared the way. I came walking alone along a gravelly shoulder under a big strip of sky, singular cliffs and buttes stretching into the distance. Whenever the sound of a car rose miles off, I drifted away from the shoulder so they would not mistake my intentions. I didn't want a ride. I was here to walk.

Pottery appeared on the ground, little gray sherds broken up by highway work. I walked a circle until I spotted a small red arrowhead. It was perfect. I picked it up, a fine piece made of jasper stone, for which I had named my first son. I held it against the sky, a fine little bird-point no bigger than a dime, something a person had knapped with great skill. You don't see many of these. *Finders keepers,* I thought. Even after all this soul-searching, this was still the first thing that came to mind. It felt as natural as a greeting: *Hello, you're mine.* You feel it when you see a coin on the sidewalk, a pearl in the sand. You reach for it and suddenly it is yours.

The arrowhead was road fill, a lost object. I knew right away that it would be a memorable marker for this day, this place on the side of the road, something I could take home. I had seen plenty of arrowheads, and they all cried out with their small voices, but this one especially. I could take it back to my son and give it to him as something to remember, a gift from his father.

Relishing it in my hand, I remembered having picked up something else that I once wanted to take home. It was a *mani* stone, an inscribed prayer from Tibet. I had found it a couple of years earlier a hundred miles from the nearest road in northeast Tibet, while navigating a remote river. I had risen early by the river's edge where our rafts were tied off, and hiked up the flank of a 17,000-foot mountain. There I found a ruined monastery, something left from hundreds of years before. Walking through its shadowy interior, among crumbled adobe walls, I came out on the other side to a shrine that was stacked with thousands of *mani* stones. The pile was chest deep, each stone a smooth, flattened river cobble about the size of a fist, with one side painstakingly carved into a prayer or a holy illustration. I picked up one that bore the image of a bodhisattva and studied the round and plump face carved there, two slits for eyes and a classic little Mona Lisa smile, something a person had scratched by hand long before my arrival. Then I picked up another, a delicate style of calligraphy reading *Om mani padme hum,* a mantra to compassion. Judging by the age of the nearby monastery, these had been gathered here over many centuries. Each felt almost warm in my hand, like a small bird.

I wanted one. What harm could there have been? They were, after all, everywhere, prayers cast into the world. I thought I could do Buddhism a favor by carrying one home, spreading the word. I had been seeing them all over the countryside, so many they tumbled down creeks. I even found them scattered among bars of natural cobbles along the river, washed downstream where they formed faint outlines of script and strokes of lotus flowers at my feet.

I let myself do it. I chose the perfect *mani* stone out of the pile, a small sunset-colored oblong with daggered Tibetan script. It was a pocket-sized masterwork. But I could not help thinking of where I was, a visitor in a region where China had recently made its big sweep, melting down artifacts so the people would forget their past. Who was I, stumbling into their history with my grabby fingers? Where did I want to put my weight in this world?

After standing still for a moment, I slid the stone back into the pile and left it there.

The story of taking or leaving artifacts is as big as China and Tibet, and as small as an arrowhead on the side of a road that I now held in my hand. It is a shared, singular longing. I was aware of what would happen if I took the arrowhead. It would likely end up in a drawer with my son's socks. It might go into my family box, clutter added to clutter, as likely to disappear as to make it through one more generation. I decided it was better here on the ground, where a person might come along and notice it, maybe next month, maybe 10,000 years from now. If those who find it leave it, the arrowhead could show itself again and again, a piece of time in a place.

I have considered the gamut of opinions, from archaeologists to dealers, from conservators to collectors, and no one has convinced me there is a better thing to do at this point than this: I flicked the arrowhead away with my thumb, and it landed back in the dirt. I left it there, wishing the earth to be populated with memory, a stone on the ground as bright as blood.

It's late and it's raining, my friends;
let's go home. Let's leave these ruins
we've haunted like owls.
                              —Rumi

ACKNOWLEDGMENTS

〜〜〜〜〜〜〜〜〜〜〜〜

My gratitude goes to friends and helpful readers, Laura Paskus, Angus Stocking, Adam Burke, and Tim Goncharoff. Thanks to the editorial direction of Geoff Shandler and Junie Dahn at Little, Brown for helping me break on through, and to my agent, Kathy Anderson, for the right suggestions at the right moments. I extend my deepest appreciation to my wife, Regan Choi, who, whether intended or not, informed every page of this book, if not every line. Finally, I am indebted to the scientists, amateurs, dealers, buyers, smugglers, conservators, curators, and diggers who trusted me, who listened, and who talked. Your candor has been critical to telling this story.

Parts of this book first appeared in different form in *High Country News*.

NOTES

~~~~~~~~~~~~~~~~

INTRODUCTION

The Matrikas of Tanesar appeared in Patrick Radden Keefe's article "The Idol Thief: Inside One of the Biggest Antiquities-Smuggling Rings in History," *The New Yorker*, May 7, 2007. Keefe reported on the movement of these statues, mentioning a trio of museums, including the Met, now in possession of three of these Matrikas.

CHAPTER 1: AMATEURS

Mention of shell trade in the prehistoric Southwest appears in much of the regional archaeological literature, and Arthur Vokes at the Arizona State Museum in Tucson is perhaps the most knowledgeable on the shells themselves. Discussing these shells, I relied on data from John W. Foster, "Shell Middens, Paleoecology, and Prehistory: The Case from Estero Morua, Sonora, Mexico," *Kiva* 41, no. 2 (1975): 185–193, and Howard Ann Valdo, "Marine Shell Artifacts and Production Processes at Shelltown and the Hind Site," in William S. Marmaduke and Richard J. Martynec, eds., *Shell Town and the Hind Site: A Study of Two Hohokam Communities in Southwestern Arizona* (Flagstaff, AZ: Northland Research, 1993). I also counted on personal communication with Michael Foster and Douglas Mitchell, both archaeologists who did field studies at the main shell source along the coast of northwest Sonora. Their findings are reported in "Hohokam Shell Middens Along the Sea of Cortez, Puerto Peñasco, Sonora, Mexico," *Journal of Field Archaeology* 27, no. 1 (2000): 27–41.

Discussion around James O. Young comes from his writings in Chris Scarre and Geoffrey Scarre, eds., *The Ethics of Archaeology: Philosophical*

Perspectives on Archaeological Practice (Cambridge: Cambridge University Press, 2006). I directed follow-up questions to Young by e-mail, and in his responses he expounded on the level of cultural value one might ascribe to an arrowhead.

Contents of the cave were inferred from the late Emil Haury's book *The Stratigraphy and Archaeology of Ventana Cave* (Tucson and Albuquerque: University of Arizona Press and University of New Mexico Press, 1950).

The case of Jack Harelson appeared widely in the press; the most detailed investigation comes from Bruce Barcott's feature "The Strange Story of Jack Harelson," which appeared in the October 2004 issue of *Outside* magazine and online at http://outside.away.com/outside/features/200410/native_america_artifacts_1.html.

The late Julian Hayden, one of the dusty and sunburned greats of Southwest archaeology, did much of the fieldwork on the Patayan culture. Background on the Patayan can be found in Jerry Schaefer's article "The Challenge of Archaeological Research in the Colorado Desert: Recent Approaches and Discoveries," *Journal of California and Great Basin Anthropology* 16, no. 1 (1994): 60–80, and in Randall H. McGuire's mainstay book *Hohokam and Patayan: Prehistory of Southwestern Arizona* (New York: Academic Press, 1982).

One of the key resources for San hunting rituals is J. D. Lewis-Williams and M. Biesele, "Eland Hunting Rituals Among Northern and Southern San Groups: Striking Similarities," *Africa* 48, no. 2 (1978): 117–134.

CHAPTER 2: THE DESTINY JAR

There is a wealth of research and academic writing on the Salado culture in the prehistoric Southwest. One of the clearest descriptions comes from Linda Cordell's *Archaeology of the Southwest* (San Diego: Academic Press, 1997).

The story of Sheng-yen and the Buddha head is, of course, far more involved than the version presented in this chapter. During my interview with him, Sheng-yen's translator explained, "He says he is also a lover of artifacts. In his travels to India and China he has been to many caves and temples, and often he has seen statues where the body is whole but the head is missing, and he says it is really sad to see that. He feels that they are actually a reflection of the beliefs of the followers of that time, and the artists. When Sheng-yen's followers gave this head to him he thought about people of that time, how they made sculptures to venerate the Buddha, and it made him sad that this head was not with its body." At the ceremony unveiling the remounted head in China, Sheng-yen had addressed the crowd: "Many people claim that 'starvation leads to theft.' In reality, this is not entirely true. People's covetous deeds and desires stem from their minds. Moreover, spiritual starvation needs to be addressed and dealt with even more than material starvation."

References to colorfully painted pottery come from Patricia L. Crown's book *Ceramics and Ideology: Salado Polychrome Pottery* (Albuquerque: University of New Mexico Press, 1994). The archaeological relevance of these polychromes was conveyed to me by personal communication with Crown (University of New Mexico) and Barbara Mills (University of Arizona).

Poisoned artifacts have been reported in numerous sources, including Merrik Bush-Pirkle, "Confronting a Tainted History," *SFSU Magazine* 1, no. 2 (Spring 2001): 11–13; Niccolo Caldararo, Lee Davis, David Hostler, Shawn Kane, and Peter Palmer, "Pesticide Testing of Hoopa Tribe Repatriated Regalia: Taking the Samples," *Collection Forum* 16, no. 63 (Summer 2001): 55–62; Lisa Goldberg, "A History of Pest Control Measures in the Anthropology Collections, National Museum of Natural History, Smithsonian Institution," *Journal of the American Institute for Conservation of Historic and Artistic Works* 35 (1996): 23–43; Micah Loma'omvaya, "NAGPRA Artifact Repatriation and Pesticides Contamination: Human Exposure to Pesticide Residue through Hopi Culture Use," presented at Special Session on Pesticides and Repatriation, International Society for Environmental Epidemiology, August 22, 2000; Micah Loma'omvaya, "NAGPRA Artifact Repatriation and Pesticides Contamination: Human Exposure to Pesticide Residue through Hopi Culture Use (Summary)," *Collection Forum* 16, no. 63 (Summer 2001): 30–37; and Nancy Odegaard and Alyce Sadongei, "The Issue of Pesticides on Native American Cultural Objects: A Report on Conservation and Education Activities at University of Arizona," *Collection Forum* 16, no. 63 (Summer 2001): 12–18. Loma'omvaya supplies the most thorough accounts, along with Nancy Odegaard's book *Old Poisons, New Problems: A Museum Resource for Managing Contaminated Cultural Materials* (Walnut Creek, CA: Alta-Mira Press, 2005).

CHAPTER 3: TREASURE HUNTERS

The relationship between archaeology and physical touch is well explored in Elizabeth Pye, ed., *The Power of Touch: Handling Objects in Museum and Heritage Contexts* (Walnut Creek, CA: Left Coast Press, 2007). In her contribution to the book, Pye describes touching antiquities: "This contact is unlike the distanced gaze of the viewer. Objects can touch us as much as we can touch them. Handling an ancient object such as a flint tool or copper alloy axe-head brings us closer to its prehistoric maker and also sends a powerful message about the maker's skill in manipulating raw material."

The case of Robert Schroeder and Newspaper Rock came from letters exchanged with Schroeder and from a report filed by the apprehending ranger.

CHAPTER 4: UNSEEN THINGS

What I consider the best reading and most up-to-date description of scientific perspectives around the Four Corners comes from Stephen Lekson, *A History of the Ancient Southwest* (Santa Fe, NM: School for Advanced Research Press, 2009).

CHAPTER 5: DIGGERS

For artifact trade out of St. Lawrence Island, I relied almost entirely on personal communication with Julie Hollowell and on her published work. Throughout the latter she maintains a readable style and a remarkably open mind. Hollowell has weathered heavy criticism for her more conservative approaches to archaeological ethics, which alone makes her work worth reading. A handful of key pieces from Hollowell are "When Archaeological Artifacts Are Commodities: Dilemmas Faced by Native Villages of Alaska's Bering Strait," in T. Peck and E. Siegfried, eds., *Indigenous People and Heritage* (Calgary, AB: University of Calgary Archaeological Association, 2003), pp. 298–312; "When Artifacts Are Commodities," in K. D. Vitelli and C. Colwell-Chanthaphonh, eds., *Archaeological Ethics* (Walnut Creek, CA: AltaMira Press, 2006); "St. Lawrence Island's Legal Market in Archaeological Goods," in N. Brodie, M. Kersel, C. Luke, and K. W. Tubb, eds., *Archaeology, Cultural Heritage, and the Antiquities Trade,* Cultural Heritage Studies Series (Gainesville: University Press of Florida, 2006), pp. 98–132; and "Ancient Ivories from the Bering Strait: Lessons from a Legal Market in Antiquities," *Athena Review* 43, no. 3 (2007): 56–66.

The late professor Andrew A. Kerr's work in southeast Utah in the 1920s comes mainly from the research of Winston Hurst. Personal communication with Hurst was crucial for much of this chapter, though his input was not sought for the 2009 raids.

Background on Earl Shumway as pothunter comes from personal communication with arresting officers and Bureau of Land Management agents who participated in a variety of investigations, as well as years of candid conversations with local residents around Bluff and Blanding, Utah.

Data on the 2009 Four Corners raid comes from unsealed affidavits, warrants, and indictments in the case, which outline the legal view of this local illicit artifact market. One warrant describes "a large ('illegal network') of individuals who regularly pillage archaeological sites, many unknown to the scientific community and many which involve funerary (burial) sites, on public land in the four corners area. Besides excavators or 'diggers', other individuals in the illegal network are dealers who buy, sell, and transport this material and collectors who are end users." The warrant goes on to explain, "The illegal network is a close knit entity. Individuals who deal in stolen archaeological objects are usually careful to disguise the site of origin. This is usually done by identifying the site of origin as leased and/or private property. Objects typically are sold with a letter of provenance which acts as a sort of title document. Letters of provenance usually list the individual who found the item, identify the location where it was found, and include assurances that the item was not illegally collected from public or Indian lands. For most transactions involved in this investigation, the Source provided a blank letter of provenance to the seller, who then represented that the artifact came from leased and/or private land. In fact, the seller recovered or knew the item was recovered on public and/or Indian land. The seller then fills out the blank letter of provenance with the false information. Further, the seller identifies for the Source on a topographic land use map, the real public land location from which the item was recovered. This is done by the seller who points to the location on the map from where the item was recovered or by circling the location on the map."

To juxtapose this strictly legal vantage, and to voice a more local, personal perspective, I relied primarily on conversations with Judy Seiler, who was ultimately advised by legal counsel to stop talking with me.

Chapter 6: Going to Market

The setting for black-market artifact trade out of Guatemala is well described in Jeremy McDermott's article "Looting a Lost Civilization," *San Francisco Chronicle,* June 7, 2001. I also relied on personal communication with David Freidel (Harvard University), Richard Hansen (Idaho State University), and William Saturno (Boston University's College of Arts and Sciences). The two stelae now in the Kimbell and Cleveland museums were reported by National Public Radio, May 28, 2007, http://www .npr.org/templates/story/story.php?storyId=10416454, and by Angela M. H. Schuster, "The Search for Site Q," *Archaeology* 50, no. 5 (September/October 1997): 42–45.

The global black market is well described by journalist Roger Atwood in his book *Stealing History: Tomb Raiders, Smugglers, and the Looting of the Ancient World* (New York: St. Martin's Press, 2004). Another important resource is Peter Watson and Cecilia Todeschini's *The Medici Conspiracy: The Illicit Journey of Looted Antiquities* (New York: PublicAffairs, 2007).

Thomas Hoving died at the age of seventy-eight, a year after I interviewed him. His story about the Euphronios krater can be found in his book *Making the Mummies Dance: Inside the Metropolitan Museum of Art* (New York: Simon and Schuster, 1993) and online in his *artnet* article "Super Art Gems of New York City," http://www.artnet.com/Magazine/FEATURES/hoving/hoving6-29-01.asp. Detailed information on the Euphronios comes from Michael Kimmelman's articles for the *New York Times,* including "Stolen Beauty: A Greek Urn's Underworld," July 7, 2009. A clear overview of the purchase history of the Euphronios can be found in Lawrence Van Gelder's *New York Times* piece "The Mysterious Trail of a Treasure, Retraced," February 5, 2006. The original heavy journalism on the subject in the 1970s came from Nicholas Gage writing for the *New York Times*.

Suzan Mazur has written extensively on Robert Hecht's involvement with the Euphronios and other pieces of antiquity.

The sale of the Guennol Lioness was reported by Maria Baugh in "Antiquities: The Hottest Investment," *Time*, December 12, 2007.

Hicham Aboutaam is frequently sought out by journalists asking about trends in the antiquities market. He gave a phone interview for this chapter. Articles used for reference include "Yemeni Stele Returns to Mideast Home," the *New York Sun*, December 2, 2004; "Hey, That's Our Art!," *BusinessWeek*, May 16, 2006; and "Out of Egypt," *St. Louis News*, February 15, 2006. An online reference to the overall state of the antiquities trade, including Aboutaam's involvement, is "Really Old Money," cnn .com, http://money.cnn.com/2008/10/23/magazines/fortune/antiquities_ hira.fortune/index.htm, last updated October 23, 2008. Phoenix Ancient Art maintains its own informative website, http://www.phoenixancientart .com/.

Key allegations in the Silk Roads Gallery case come from the unsealed warrant. Jason Felch, staff writer for the *Los Angeles Times*, did most of the reporting, including "Raids Suggest a Deeper Network of Looted Art," January 25, 2008, and "Intrigue but No Glamour for Smuggling Case Figure," January 31, 2008. Felch also reported on Roxanna Brown's case and her death in "A Scholar's Journey Leads through War, Addiction and Injury to Arrest," September 11, 2008, and "Her Career Revived, Scholar Turns Tipster," September 12, 2008. Other useful articles came from Edward Wyatt writing for the *New York Times*. Details of communication between Brown and other players in the Silk Roads Gallery case, including letters and e-mails, were photocopied and attached to the original warrant.

An interview with Fred Brown supplied the conclusion to this chapter as he defended his deceased sister's reputation. After her death, the case surrounding the Silk Roads Gallery came to an apparent standstill, and a year later, the U.S. attorney's office in Seattle, Washington, settled a lawsuit with Brown's family, paying $880,000 to her estate. The further fallout from this probe is described in Edward Wyatt's article "Papers Show Wider Focus in Inquiry of Artifacts," *New York Times*, January 30, 2008.

Chapter 7: A History of Urges

Personal communication with Dr. Wang Jiqing, Lanzhou University, Gansu Province, China, provided necessary background on Wang Yuanlu.

Piecing together the story of Aurel Stein in the Taklamakan, I relied on several secondary sources, including Christoph Baumer, *Southern Silk Road: In the Footsteps of Sir Aurel Stein and Sven Hedin* (Bangkok: White

Orchid Books, 2000); Jeannette Mirsky, *Sir Aurel Stein: Archaeological Explorer* (Chicago: University of Chicago Press, 1998); Peter Hopkirk, *Foreign Devils on the Silk Road: The Search for the Lost Cities and Treasures of Chinese Central Asia* (Amherst: University of Massachusetts Press, 1984); and Susan Whitfield, *Aurel Stein on the Silk Road* (Chicago: Serindia Publications, 2004).

Original documentation about Stein's travels came from reports authored by Stein himself: *Ancient Khotan: Detailed Report of Archaeological Explorations in Chinese Turkestan*, 2 vols., reprint (Oxford: Clarendon Press, 1907); *Sand-Buried Ruins of Khotan: Personal Narrative of a Journey of Archaeological and Geographical Exploration in Chinese Turkestan* (London: Hurst, 1904); *Ruins of Desert Cathay: Personal Narrative of Explorations in Central Asia and Westernmost China* (London: Macmillan, 1912); *Preliminary Report on a Journey of Archaeological and Topographical Exploration in Chinese Turkestan* (London: Eyre and Spottiswoode, 1901); and *The Thousand Buddhas: Ancient Buddhist Paintings from the Cave-Temples of Tun-huang on the Western Frontier of China, Recovered and Described by Aurel Stein* (London: Quaritch, 1921).

An important overview of the art in the Caves of the Thousand Buddhas can be found in Roderick Whitfield's *Caves of the Singing Sands: Buddhist Art from the Silk Road* (London: Textile and Art Publications, 1995). I also took some of the description of individual murals from plates in *The Sacred Oasis: Caves of the Thousand Buddhas, Tun Huang* (London: Faber & Faber, 1953).

The International Dunhuang Project has an excellent website for both the history of the caves and detailed investigation of what was found in them at http://idp.bl.uk/.

China's increased purchasing power is reported by Souren Melikian in "Chinese Bidders Conquer Market," *New York Times,* April 2, 2010.

Chapter 8: The Chosen Ones

Randall McGuire wrote about his experience as an archaeologist in Mexico in an essay entitled "The Gringo Stigma" in K. D. Vitelli and C. Colwell-Chanthaphonh, eds., *Archaeological Ethics* (Walnut Creek, CA: AltaMira Press, 2006). This particular book is an excellent compendium of sometimes conflicting perspectives that have been published by scholars and journalists in *Archaeology* magazine, and McGuire's chapter is the book's most candid explanation of an archaeologist's point of view.

Michael Shanks's quote comes from his book *Experiencing the Past: On the Character of Archaeology* (London and New York: Routledge, 1992).

Charles Bowden's quote comes from a book he published with photographer Michael Berman, *Inferno* (Austin: University of Texas Press, 2006).

Accounts of Gustaf Nordenskiöld are from original newspaper sources and Judith and David Reynolds, *Nordenskiöld of Mesa Verde* (Xlibris, 2006).

The quote from Layton and Wallace comes from their chapter "Is Culture a Commodity?" in Chris Scarre and Geoffrey Scarre, eds., *The Ethics of Archaeology: Philosophical Perspectives on Archaeological Practice* (Cambridge: Cambridge University Press, 2006).

In 2000, the Society for American Archaeology laid out ethical principles for archaeologists: "The archaeological record, that is, in situ archaeological materials and sites, archaeological collections, records, and reports, is irreplaceable. It is the responsibility of all archaeologists to work for the long-term conservation and protection of the archaeological record by practicing and promoting stewardship of the archaeological record. Stewards are both caretakers and advocates for the archaeological record for the benefit of all people; as they investigate and interpret the record, they should use the specialized knowledge they gain to promote understanding and support for its long-term preservation."

Though this preamble sounds watertight, its focus on stewardship by professional archaeologists has been questioned. Leo Groarke and Gary Warrick, writing in Chris Scarre and Geoffrey Scarre, eds., *The Ethics of Archaeology: Philosophical Perspectives on Archaeological Practice* (Cambridge: Cambridge University Press, 2006), say, "The problem is that the SAA principle does not clearly identify [the] owners, and in this way fails to identify the 'master' whose interest will determine the obligations of the archaeologist-as-steward."

Great Plains archaeologist Jason LaBelle adds, in Larry J. Zimmerman, Karen D. Vitelli, and Julie Hollowell-Zimmer, eds., *Ethical Issues in Archaeology* (Walnut Creek, CA: AltaMira Press and Society for American Archaeology, 2003): "Although some might think otherwise, the past clearly does not belong to a chosen few with university degrees, but instead belongs to a rich patchwork of communities, including the people who left the material originally, their descendants, the modern local community (including collectors), and interested researchers, who often are from very distant lands, both politically and geographically. Developing a dialog with all of these groups certainly strengthens our discipline as a whole."

Chip Colwell-Chanthaphonh and T. J. Ferguson, two leading voices in the realm of archaeology, ethics, and Native America, emphasize, "Despite the significant shift in power stemming from ownership and control of important parts of the archaeological record, archaeologists in the United States are still allotted more control and power over heritage resources and the past they represent than any other group." This appeared in a chapter they coauthored in K. D. Vitelli and C. Colwell-Chanthaphonh, eds., *Archaeological Ethics* (Walnut Creek, CA: AltaMira Press, 2006).

George Peabody's comments came from *Reports of the Peabody Museum of American Archaeology and Ethnology in Connection*

NOTES

with Harvard University, vol. 1, 1868–1876 (Salem, MA: Salem Press, 1876).

Numbers of artifacts in storage were derived from *A Public Trust at Risk: The Heritage Health Index Report on the State of America's Collections* (Washington, D.C.: Heritage Preservation, 2005). This is the first comprehensive survey ever conducted of the condition and preservation needs of all U.S. collections held in the public trust, and it offers a sweeping but detailed perspective of what is happening inside public collections.

Frederick Matthew Wiseman's response to the current archaeological hierarchy can be found in his book *The Voice of the Dawn* (Hanover, NH: University Press of New England, 2001).

CHAPTER 9: SALVAGE ARCHAEOLOGY

Philosopher Geoffrey Scarre's quote about taking liberties with the dead comes from the book he edited with his brother, the archaeologist Chris Scarre, *The Ethics of Archaeology: Philosophical Perspectives on Archaeological Practice* (Cambridge: Cambridge University Press, 2006). A predominantly academic book, this is a primary resource, its contributors offering some of the best writing on the deeper philosophical issues surrounding archaeology. More than any other, this book gets at the heart of the matter of who rightfully owns the past and how professionals deal with ensuing dilemmas.

CHAPTER 10: THE GOLDEN JAR

Ron Stodghill's March 18, 2007, *New York Times* piece "Do You Know Where That Art Has Been?" details the discovery and sale of Apollo the Lizard Slayer. Another useful article on the subject is Steven Litt's September 12, 2004, *Cleveland Plain Dealer* article "A God of Myth Cloaked in Mystery."

The finding of repainted, refired vessels comes from personal communication with Patty Crown and an article she wrote with W. H. Wills, "Modifying Pottery and Kivas at Chaco: Pentimento, Restoration, or Renewal?," in *American Antiquity* 68, no. 3 (2003): 511–532.

CHAPTER 11: HOUSES OF OBSESSION

Charles Stanish argues that Internet sales of antiquities have actually reduced looting in "Forging Ahead: Or, How I Learned to Stop Worrying and Love eBay," *Archaeology* 64, no. 3 (May/June 2009), also found at http://www.archaeology.org/0905/etc/insider.html. Arguments against his notion soon appeared in blogs, including Larry Rothfield's The Punching Bag, http://www.blogcatalog.com/blog/safecorner-cultural-heritage-in-danger/e637d51a1ee52e51a7b7c5410c3eb116, where Rothfield wrote,

"On a quick first read, it seems logically persuasive, with some caveats. One is that if eBay is expanding the market then even if fakes bring the prices down relative to what a market with lower level of supply would charge, the increase in the number of potential buyers might drive the price back up, leaving the incentive to loot about what it was before."

Cornelius Holtorf's quote comes from his book *From Stonehenge to Las Vegas: Archaeology as Popular Culture* (Walnut Creek, CA: AltaMira Press, 2004), a refreshingly unique perspective on the ownership of the past.

The case for private collection as well as criticism of the 1970 UNESCO treaty can be read in George Ortiz's chapter in Eleanor Robson, Luke Treadwell, and Chris Gosden, eds., *Who Owns Objects: The Ethics and Politics of Collecting Cultural Artefacts* (Oxford: Oxbow Books, 2006). This book offers an excellent overview of arguments for and against collection, both private and public.

The concept of historicity is adeptly explored by author James Gleick in his January 6, 2008, *New York Times* article "Keeping It Real," where Gleick considers the underlying value of an authentic Magna Carta copy selling for $21.3 million. He writes, "The value of the particular item sold at Sotheby's eight centuries later is...a kind of illusion. We can call it magical value as opposed to meaningful value."

Souren Melikian's quote comes from his January 17, 1998, *New York Times* article, "Some Solutions to the Looting of Cultures: On the Eve of Destruction?"

CHAPTER 12: PUBLIC TRUST

Several museums around the country generously allowed me into their vaults, which offered a general comparison between institutions. This chapter focused primarily on the Peabody Museum of Archaeology and Ethnology, where Susan Haskell was my main source, having allowed me in, as was the case with other museums I visited, under museum protocol.

Background on the Awat'ovi site and its murals comes from Watson Smith's *Kiva Murals and Decorations at Awatovi and Kwawika-A* (Cambridge, MA: Peabody Museum of Archaeology and Ethnology, 1952).

This account of artifacts in storage comes from *A Public Trust at Risk: The Heritage Health Index Report on the State of America's Collections* (Washington, D.C.: Heritage Preservation, 2005).

Discussion of the looting of the National Museum of Iraq comes from personal communication with its former curator Donny George Youkhanna and from numerous news reports. A well-written and thorough book on the subject, for a popular audience, is Matthew Bogdanos's *Thieves of Baghdad* (New York: Bloomsbury, 2005).

NOTES

CHAPTER 13: NO PLACE LIKE HOME

Again, Cornelius Holtorf's quotes are from his book *From Stonehenge to Las Vegas.*

Systematic cultural destruction that occurred in Tibet is compiled in Rebecca Knuth's book *Libricide: The Regime-Sponsored Destruction of Books and Libraries in the Twentieth Century* (Westport, CT: Praeger, 2003). The discussion about the Jowo Shakymuni relied in part on personal communication with Cameron Warner, a Tibetologist who received his PhD from the Department of Sanskrit and Indian Studies at Harvard.

Siân Jones, a Scottish archaeologist, has done a wonderful job of bringing in local and historical perspectives on the Cadboll Stone. A starting place for Jones's work is her book *Early Medieval Sculpture and the Production of Meaning, Value and Place: The Case of Hilton of Cadboll* (Edinburgh: Historic Scotland, 2004).

CHAPTER 14: HOLDING ON

This chapter relies entirely on personal communication with Forrest Fenn. Asking him to set forth his attitude about private antiquities ownership, I followed Fenn around with a recorder for a day as we explored his collection of drawers and boxes, and his vault.

CHAPTER 15: LETTING GO

Again, this chapter comes wholly from personal communication and experience.

CODA

The 2009 case of antiquities found in a Chicago bungalow appears in an online FBI press release, http://www.fbi.gov/page2/june09/artifacts061109.html, and in a June 9, 2009, *Chicago Tribune* article entitled "1600 Antiquities for Italy: FBI Sending Back Stolen Artifacts Found in Berwyn," by Margaret Ramirez and Robert Mitchum.

INDEX

Peabody Museum of Archaeology
  and Ethnology (Cambridge,
  Massachusetts), 41, 136, 188–92,
  194, 196, 201–3, 211
  Hopi ceremonial rites held in, 193
  repatriation of artifacts by, 197
People magazine, 221
Petén region. *See* Guatemala
petroglyphs. *See* rock art
Phoenix, Arizona, artifacts from, 155–56.
  See also American Southwest
Phoenix Ancient Art (New York and
  Geneva), 108–11
Plains people, 224. *See also* Native
  American culture
Pliny the Elder, 163
poisoned artifacts, 41–43, 136
Pompeii, artifacts from, 224. *See also*
  Italy, artifacts from
pothunters, 79, 85, 173–76
  and drug trade, 80, 235
  as part of history, 46
  Utah raids of, 83–84, 86, 87–94
  See also diggers
Praxiteles (Greek sculptor), 163–64
pre-Columbian times, 222
  artifacts from, *see* artifacts
prices. *See* artifacts (market prices)
provenance, 102, 108, 110
  doubtful, 114, 135, 178; and return of
    artifacts, 111 (*see also* repatriation)
  of Euphronios krater, 103–5
  letters of, 257
  of private collections, 179, 223
Pueblo people. *See* Native American
  culture

raids, government. *See* United States
Ramos Polychrome style, 167, 180
Ramses II, statue of, 153. *See also* Egypt
Redd family, 88, 89, 93
repatriation
  of Aphrodite sculpture, 106, 197
  of Chinese relics, 38, 131
  demands for, 5, 98–99, 115, 136, 163,
    197, 210
  doubtful provenance and, 111
  of Euphronios krater, 105–6, 197
  of Iraqi artifacts looted from National
    Museum, 111–12, 199–200
  Native American push for, 136–37, 197
  of poisoned artifacts, 41–43, 136
  of pre-Columbian artifacts,
    155–56, 178

repatriation laws, 5, 41–43, 136–37, 197
  replica sent to Guatemala, 98–99
  of Salado pot, 37–41, 43–49, 144
  of Sumerian statue, 111–12
  of Thai antiquities, 115
  of Tibetan artifacts, 208
replicas of artifacts. *See* artifacts
rituals. *See* ceremonial sites and artifacts
rock art (petroglyphs), 51–52, 53, 236
Rodriguez, Anibal, 203
Roman burial sites in London, 153
Roman sculpture fragment found in
  Mexican grave, 168
Russian archaeologists in China, 128

sacrificial sites, 216–18. *See also*
  ceremonial sites and artifacts
Sagebrush Rebellion, 82
Salado people. *See* Native
  American culture
sandals, oldest pair of, 23
San Juan County, Utah, 78, 80, 84
San people (South Africa), 26
Saturno, William, 97–98, 211–14, 226
Scarre, Geoffrey, 158
Schroeder, Robert, 51–52, 53, 54
Scotland, Cadboll Stone in, 209–10, 219
seashells in the desert, 16–17
seed jars, 55–58
Seiler, Judy, 91–92, 93–94
Shanks, Michael, 138
Sheng-yen (Zen master), 38
Sheridan, General Philip, 228
"shovel bums," 153. *See also* archaeology
Shrader, Steven, 90, 92
shrines, 8, 25–30, 62. *See also* burial sites
Shrivastava, Anand, 7–8
Shumway, Earl, 82–84, 87–88, 95,
  138, 236
Shumway family, 81–82, 88
Siberia, 75, 76
Sicily, sculpture repatriated to, 106
Sierra Madre, 164, 179, 203
Silk Road, the, 121
Silk Roads Gallery (Los Angeles), 113–18
Sitting Bull's pipe, 227–29
Smithsonian Institution, 41, 194
smuggling and smuggling rings, 8, 95–96,
  105, 111–12, 113–18, 178, 200
  and Euphronios krater, 103–5
  UNESCO antismuggling treaty, *see*
    UNESCO Convention
Society for American Archaeology (SAA),
  135, 260

Sonderman, Bob, 141–42
Sotheby's auction house, 107–8, 109
South American sites plundered, 99
Southeast Asian Ceramics Museum
  (Bangkok), 115, 117
Southern Ute people, 92. *See also* Native
  American culture
Southwest. *See* American Southwest
staffs, wooden, 236–37
Stanish, Charles, 180
St. Christopher medal, 201
Stein, Aurel, 123–31, 133, 134, 145, 147
stelae cut apart, 98–99
stewardship, 135–37, 185, 260. *See also*
  ethical questions
St. Lawrence Island (Alaska), 75–78, 81
Stone Age, 23
Stonehenge, 218
Strater Hotel (Durango, Colorado), 90, 147
Sumerian artifacts, 109
  looted from Iraq, 111–12, 198;
  returned, 112
Susan (writer), 62–71
Sweden, in Nordenskiöld case, 147
Swedish Museum of Natural History, 145
Switzerland, 100, 104–5, 110
Syria, 109, 111

Taj Mahal, 119
Taklamakan Desert, 120–21, 123–24,
  126, 203
Taoist tradition, 121
Tasmanian Aborigines, return demands
  by, 136
Temple of Dendur (Egypt), 218. *See
  also* Egypt
Teotihuacán (pre-Columbian city), 75
Texsun can, 45, 48
Thailand, 113–15, 117–18
thefts from museums, 197–99
Third World environment, 96
Tibet, 27, 34, 120
  China destroys artifacts of, 208–9, 247
  Jowo Shakymuni statue, 208–9, 218
  mani stones from, 246–47
Tiffany & Co., 101
Time magazine, 108
True, Marion, 106
Tsosie, Will, 44, 239
Tutankhamen, King, 68–69

Ugly Man, 29–31, 232
UNESCO Convention on the Means
  of Prohibiting and Preventing the

Illicit Import, Export and Transfer
  of Ownership of Cultural Property,
  101–2, 103–5, 109
United States
  antiquities laws in, *see* laws and
    legislation
  archaeologist in China, 128–29
  Army Corps of Engineers, 141
  black market for artifacts, 97
  Bureau of Land Management (BLM),
    91, 93, 223, 236
  buyers and collectors, 100
  catalogued objects in public trust, 142,
    194, 261
  Department of Homeland
    Security, 110
  Department of the Interior, 92
  government digs and surveys, 8, 148
  government raids of looters, collectors,
    and dealers, 6, 24, 83–94, 113–18,
    147, 178, 183, 223; Cerberus Action,
    89–94
  invades Iraq, 111, Baghdad, 198–200
  returns Mexican artifacts, 178
  National Park Service, 141, 194
  and UNESCO Convention, 104
  See also American Northwest;
    American Southwest; North
    America
University of Arizona, 137, 140
University of California, Los
  Angeles, Department of
  Anthropology, 180
University of Durham (England), 158
University of Lund (Sweden), 43
University of New Mexico, 169, 194
University of Pennsylvania Museum, 114
University of Victoria (Canada), 18
URS (United Research Services), 156
Utah. *See* American Southwest

vandalism, 166, 184
  vs. renewal, 169–70
  See also looting
Varien, Mark, 142–43
Ventana Cave (Arizona), 23. *See
  also* caves
Vietnam War, 225
von Bothmer, Dietrich, 103–5

Wallace, Gillian, 150
Wang Yuanlu, 120–22, 124–30, 131
Washington State, Kennewick Man from,
  136–37